STO

AC
DISCARDED

P9-EDT-050

MAY 19 '76

ENGLISH RECUSANT LITERATURE
1558–1640

Selected and Edited by
D. M. ROGERS

Volume 291

ALFONSO RODRIGUEZ
A Treatise of Mentall Prayer
1627

ALFONSO RODRIGUEZ
A Treatise of Mentall Prayer
1627

The Scolar Press
1976

ISBN 0 85967 292 1

Published and printed in Great Britain by
The Scolar Press Limited, 59-61 East Parade,
Ilkley, Yorkshire and
39 Great Russell Street,
London WC1

1900745

NOTE

Reproduced (original size) from a copy in Cambridge University Library, by permission of the Syndics. A blemish in the lower half of page 60 has caused slight loss of text. The relevant passage reads: '. . . any more then if he belieued it not. He bindes vp his eyes; which comes to the same reckoning for him, as if he were blind.'

References: Allison and Rogers 737; STC 21148.

A TREATISE

Of Mentall Prayer.

WITH ANOTHER
Of the Presence of God.

Composed by the R. Fa. A L-
FONSVS RODRIGVEZ, of the
Society of IESVS.

nowship AND

Translated out of the Spanish,
into English.

Permissu Superiorum. 1627.

TO THE
RIGHT REVEREND
LADY ABBESSE

*Of the English Religious
Dames, of the Order of
S. Benet in Gant.*

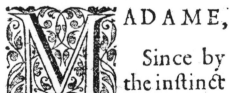ADAME,

Since by
the inſtinct
of *Nature*,
all things acknovvledge
the *Fountayne*, vvhence
originally they flovv : I

★ 2   should

should haue vvronged this Excellent *TREA-TISE*, had I directed the fame , into any other , then your *LADIS-HIPPS* Hands , from vvhome I firſt receaued it ; and to vvhome, by the *TRANSLA-TOVRS Intention* , and for many other reſpects , it is ſingularly due .

And although, this be but a ſmall *Part* , or one ſingle *Tracte* only , of the admirable *VVOR-KES* of the *Authour*; yet hath

hath it byn iudged fit, to be published alone ; to the end the pious *Reader* may not be depriued of so *Excellent* a *Treasure*, vntill the *VVhole* may come to light . And I doubt not , but that the printing of this , vvilbe no small *Motiue* to the *VVorthy* *TRANS-LATOVR*, to go forvvard vvith the rest ; seeing his former Deuout *Labours*, in furthering of Spirituall *Matters* , are highly esteemed , & ho-

★ 3   noured

noured by all pious, and vnpartiall Readers therof.

In this Treatise (*MADAME*) may the Deuout *Contemplant*, read vvithout *VVearinesse*, & repeat vvithout *Tediousnesse*; sucking euermore from hence, most svveet *Delightes* of Diuine *Cōfort*; the vvhich do so satiate, as they procure also nevv *Appetite*, in those, vvho addict themselues to the practice of *MENTAL PRAYER*.

For,

DEDICATORY.

For, amongſt all the *Spirituall BOOKES*, novv extant, I knovv not any one, more generally *Applauded*, or accounted more *Neceſſary*, for ſuch, as attend to the deuout Exerciſe of *Prayer*, then this : The *AUTHOVR* vvherof, hauing byn not only trayned vp, all his life tyme, in the *Schoole* of *VERTUE*; but alſo, one of the moſt expert *Maiſters* of *SPIRIT*, that are knovvne, at this day,

* 4   in

in the Christian vvorld.

Vnto this *Tracte* of *MENTAL PRAY-ER*, haue I adioyned another more briefe, *Of the Presence of God*, made by the same *AVTHOVR*. For, as these tvvo pious *Exercises*, haue such dependance one of the other, that they cannot be separated in *Practice*: So vvas it thought conuenient, to combine them togeather in one *Booke*; that the same might be more entierely *vsefull*,

for

for the arriuing vnto a
true, and perfect *Spirit* of
Deuotion, & *Union* vvith
God.

I vvill not enter into
further *Difcourfe*, in pray-
fe heerof; as vvell, not to
be ouer-tedious to your
L A D I S H I P P E; as
not to hinder you from
enioying the fvveet *Con-
tent*, vvhich you vvill (no
doubt) receaue, by the
Perufall. As for the fmall
Paines, I may haue taken
in the publishing of it,
the *Benefit* vvhich many
foules

THE EPISTLE

foules vvill reape heere-
by, shalbe my *Comfort*;
and my poore *Prayers*
shall euer be attending
You, for the perpetuall
Increase of your spirituall *Happines*: Whereof
I humbly befeech You,
to make him Partaker,
vvho hath dedicated
Himfelfe, to remayne
euer,

Your La.ᵖ. *deuoted*
Seruant.

I. W.

A TABLE
OF THE CONTENTS
of this Booke.

Of Mentall Prayer.

THE TABLE.

CHAP.

THE TABLE.

CHAP.

THE TABLE.

Of the presence of God:

Chap. I.

OF *the excellency of this* Exercise: *and the great benefits, which are conteyned therein.* Pag. 261.

Chap. II.
Wherein consisteth the Exercise, *or* Practise *of going alwayes, in the* Presence of God. Pag. 273.

Chap. III.
Of the Acts of the Will, wherein this Exercise doth principally consist; and how we

are

THE TABLE.

Of

Of Mentall Prayer.

CHAP. I.

Of the Value, and Excellency of Prayer.

THE glorious Apostle, and Euangelist *S. Iohn*, in the fifth, & eight Chapters of his *Apocalyps*, doth well declare the value and excellency of Prayer, and sayth: *That the Angell stood before the Altar and held an Incensary of Gold in his hand; and that a great quantity of Incense was giuen to him, which were the Prayers of the Saints; to the end, that he might offer them vp before the Altar of Gold, which stood before the Throne of God: and that the smoke of that Incense, did ascend, from the*

A   *hand*

hand of that *Angell*, into the preſence of God.
S. Chryſoſtome ſpeaking vpon this place

Chryſ.ho.
13. ſuper
Matth. in
opere im-
perfect.

ſayth: Hereby you may diſcerne how
high & pretious a thing *Prayer* is, ſince
it alone, is compared in holy Scripture
to *Thymiama*, which was a confection
of Incenſe, and other things, moſt o-
doriferouſly fragrant. Becauſe, as *Thymiama*, being well compounded, and
framed, did extraordinarily delight mē
by the odour of it; ſo that *Prayer*, which
is made, as it ought, is very ſweet and
and pleaſing to Almighty God; and
doth delight and recreate the holy Angells, and all the other Cittizens of

Guiller.
Pariſ. in
ſua Rheto.
diſti. c. 4.

Heauen. In ſuch ſorte, as that *S. Iohn*
ſayth, They haue in their hands, as it
were ſo many pomanders of admirable odour, which are the Prayers of the
Saints; wherunto they do very often
apply their moſt pure ſent, (to ſpeake
after the manner of men) that ſo they
may enioy this moſt ſweet ſmell: *Ha-
bentes ſinguli, Phialas aureas, plenas odora-
mentorum, quæ ſunt orationes Sanctorum.*

Aug. in
tract. de
miſericor.
Tom. 10.

　　S. Auguſtine ſpeaking of Prayer ſaith:
*Quid eſt oratione clarius? quid vitæ noſtræ
vtilius? quid animo dulcius? quid in tota no-
ſtra*

neſtra religione ſublimius ? What thing
is there more excellent ? What more
profitable? what more delightful, and
ſweet? what more ſublyme, and high
in all our Chriſtian Religion , then
Prayer? *S. Gregory* of *Nice* , ſayth the
ſame : *Nihil ex his, quæ per hanc vitam co-*
luntur & in precio ſunt, oratione præſtat.

Greg. Niſ-
ſen. de orat.
Dom. in.

S. *Bernard* ſayth, That although it
be certaine, that the Angells do very
ordinarily aſſiſt the ſeruants of God
with their inuiſible preſence, ſo to deliuer them from the fraudes & ſleights
of the Enemy, and to ſet forward their
deſires of ſeruing God , with greater
feruour: Yet much more aſſiſtance do
thoſe Angelicall ſpirits giue, when we
imploy our ſelues, in making *Prayer.*
And he bringeth to this purpoſe, many
places of Holy Scripture; as that of the
Pſalmiſt, *In conſpectu Angelorum pſallam*
tibi: I will praiſe thee, in the preſence
of the Angells. *Præuenerunt Principes con-*
iuncti pſalientibus , in medio inuencularum
tympaniſtriarum; which he alſo declareth
of the Angells, who aſſociate themſelues to ſuch as pray. And that alſo,
which the Angell ſaid to *Tobias: When*

Ber. ſer. 7.
ſuper Cāt.
& *Ep.* 78.

Pſal. 137.

Pſal. 67.

Tob. 12.
12.

A 2 *thou*

thou didst pray with tears, I offered vp thy Prayers to God. For when the Prayer issueth out of his mouth who maketh it; iust then, do the Angells, who are preset, offer it vp to God. *S. Hilary* sayth the same thing: *Angeli præsunt fidelium orationibus, & eas quotidie Deo offerunt.* So that when we be in Prayer, we are inuironed, and circled in by Angells; & our selues are also doing the office of Angells; and we are practising, and exercising our selues in that, which hereafter we are to do continually in Heauen, and that is, to blesse & praise our Lord. And for this cause, we are particulerly fauoured, and beloued by the Angells, as being their Companions now, & being also expected to be so hereafter; filling vp those seates, which grew empty, by the fall of their fellowes.

S. Chrysostome, treating of the excellency of *Prayer*, and being desirous to expresse the greatnesse of it, sayth: That one of the highest greatnesses which did occur to be expressed by him, was this, That whosoeuer maketh *Prayer*, doth confer, and treate with God himselfe;

Hilar. can. 18. in Mat.

Chrys. lib. 2. de oran- do Deum.

selfe: *Considera quanta est tibi conceßa fælicitas, quanta gloria attributa, orationibus fabulari cum Deo; cum Christo miscere colloquia; optare quod velis; quod desideras postulare.* Conſider the dignity, & the glory to which our Lord nath exalted tnee, in that he hath giuen thee power, to treate and conuerſe with him; to haue conuerſation, & ſpeach of intercourſe with Ieſus Chriſt; to deſire what thou wilt, and to aske what thou deſyreſt. *There is no tongue* (ſayth he) *which can a-riue to declare of how great dignity, & height, this treating and conuerſing is, with Almighty God; and of how great vſe and profit to vs.* For if they, who haue their ordinary conuerſation here on earth, with wiſe and prudent men, do feele much profit in ſhort tyme; & it growes quickly to be knowne, that they are much im-proued in wiſdome, & knowledge; & if they, who hold familiarity with vertuous men, do ſucke of that vertue into themſelues, (as the Prouerbe doth thus expreſſe) *Conuerſe with good men, & thy ſelfe wilt growe to be one of them;* what ſhall become of ſuch perſons, as con-uerſe & treate, in frequent, & familiar

man-

Psa. 33.

manner, with Almighty God? *Accedite ad Deum & illuminamini* . What light, & knowledge, what benefits and benedictions, will they receaue by such cōuersation, and communication as this? And so S. *Chrysostome* sayth: That there is nothing, which maketh vs so much growe in vertue, as much *Prayer*, and frequent conuersation with Almighty God. For thus the hart of man, growes to be truly generous, and to haue the things of this world in great cōtempt; and to raise himselfe aboue them all; and to vnite, and transforme himselfe, after a certaine manner, into God; and to become, in fine, a spirituall person, and a Saint .

*Chrysos.
ho. ae orat.
& super
illud Ps 7.
Confite-
bor Do-
mino se-
cundum
Iustitiam
eius.*

Chap. II.

Of the great Necessity, which we haue of Prayer.

HOvv necessary *Prayer* is for vs, we haue inough, & inough experience. I would to God (if he were so pleased,) that we had not so much . Now, since man is so full of need of

Gods

Gods fauour, in respect that he is subiect to the taking of so many falls ; and
that he is inuironed by so many, and so
fierce enemyes ; and laboureth vnder
the want of so many things, which belong aswell to the soule as the body;
there remaines no other remedy for
him, but euer to be resorting to God; beseeching him, with his whole hart, to
be fauourable to him, and that he will
help him out of all his dangers, & ne-
cessities, according to that which King *2. Paral.*
Iosaphat said (whē he foūd himself hem'd *10. 2.*
in by his enemyes:) *Cùm ignoremus quid*
agere debeamus , hoc solùm habemus residui ,
vt oculos nostros dirigamus ad te. Since we
are so weake , since we are so poore,
and needy, and know not which way
to turne our selues, we haue no other
remedy, but onely to cast vp our eyes
to God , and with our harts to beg of *Celest. ca.*
him , those things wherof we are in so *9. contra*
great neede. And so Pope *Celestine*, in *Pelagium.*
one of his Decretall Epistles , to teach
the importance of Prayer , speaketh
thus; I know not what better thing to
say to you, then that which *Zozimus* my
Predecessour sayd, *Quod est tempus, in quo*
eius

*eius auxilio non indigemus? in omnibus igitur
rebus, causis, & negotijs, exorandus est Pro-
tector Deus.* What tyme is there, wherein we haue not neceſſity of the help of
God? There is no ſuch tyme. If that
be ſo, then are we, at all tymes, and
in all occaſions, and in all affayres, to
reſort to God by Prayer, with deſyre
that he will protect vs. *Superbū eſt enim,
vt humana natura aliquid de ſe praſumat.*
For a great pride it is, that a frayle and
miſerable man, ſhould preſume any
litle vpon himſelfe.

<table>
<tr><td>

S. Tho. 2. 2.
q. 81. ar. 2.
Damaſc. l.
3. *fidei ca.*
2 4. *Aug.*
l. 2. de ſer.
Domini
cap 7. &
ſer. 230. de
temp.
Baſilius in
Iul. mart.
Chryſ. ho.
30. *in Ge-*
neſim. Gre.
l. 2. dial.
c. 8.

</td><td>

S. *Thomas* proues the neceſſity of
Prayer, by a very ſolide, and ſubſtan-
tiall reaſon; and it is the doctrine of the
Saints *Damaſcen, Auguſtine, Baſill, Chry-
ſoſtome,* and *Gregory.* Theſe Saints de-
clare, that the things which God, by
his diuine wiſdom and diſpoſition, did
determine, from all *Eternity,* to giue to
ſoules; he would impart in time, by
meanes of *Prayer*; and that by this mea-
nes, he had reſolued vpon the redreſſe,
the conuerſion, and the ſaluation of
many ſoules; and vpon the progreſſe,
and perfection of many others: in ſuch
ſort, that as God diſpoſed and deter-
mined,

</td></tr>
</table>
mined,

mined, that by meanes of marriage,
mankind should be multiplyed ; and
that by plowing, and sowing , & cul-
tiuating the ground otherwise , there
should grow abundance of bread, and
wine, and other fruits of the earth ; and
that, by meanes of Artificers , and ma-
terialls, houses , and buildings should
be erected : So did he also ordayne to
worke great effects in the world , and
to communicate many graces & guifts
to soules, by this meanes of *Prayer.* And
so did Christ our Redeemer assure vs, in
the Ghospell: *Petite & dabitur vobis, quæ-*
rite & inuenietis , pulsate & aperietur vobis : Matt. 7.
omnis enim qui petit, accipit , & qui quærit ,
inuenit, & pulsanti aperitur. Aske and it
shalbe giuen, seeke and you shall finde,
knock and it shalbe opened vnto you :
for he who asketh receyueth , he who
seeketh findeth , & to him who knoc-
keth , it shalbe opened.

So that *Prayer,* is the meanes & mai-
ster-conduit , wherby our Lord wilbe
pleased to releiue our necessityes , to
inrich our pouerty ; & to replenish vs
with benedictions and graces. Wherby
we see well, the great necessity which
we

we haue of frequenting *Prayer*. And so
the Saints do frame, a very fit comparison, when they affirme, that *Prayer* is
as a *chayne* of Gold, one end wherof is
hooked vp in heauen, & the other end
reacheth downe to the earth; and that,
by this *chayne*, all celestiall graces, are
deriued, and drawne downe to vs; and
by the same, our selues ascend, & mout
vp to God. And we may also say, that
this is a kind of *Iacobs* Ladder, *which
reacheth from heauen to earth; and wherby
the Angells do ascend, and descend.*

*Gen.*28.
12.
Aug.ser.
226.

The glorious *S. Augustine* sayth, that
Prayer is the *Key of Heauen*, which is
made, to open all the gates therof; and
of all those coffers which are full of
the treasures of God, without excep-
ting any one. *Oratio iusti, clauis est cæli:
ascendit precatio, & descendit Dei miseratio.*
And els where he sayth: That looke
what breade is to the body, that very
thing is Prayer to the soule: *Sicut ex
carnalibus escis alitur caro, ita ex diuinis elo-
quijs & orationibus, interior homo nutritur,
& pascitur.* And the same is affirmed,
by the holy Martyr, & Abbot *Nilus.*

*Aug ex-
hort. de
salutari-
bus moni-
tis ad quē-
dam Co-
mitem ca.*
28.
Nilus ca.
95. de orat.
in bib. SS.
PP. 10. 3.

One of the most principall considerations,

derations, wherby the Saintes declare
the value, and estimation which we
ought to make of *Prayer*, on the one
side; and on the other, the great necessity which we haue therof; is, because
Prayer, is a very principall, and efficacious meanes, to order and addresse our
life, and to explayne, or ouercome all
those difficultyes, which may offer
themselues to vs, in the way of vertue.
And so they say, that vpon it, depends
the gouermēt of our life; & that when
Prayer is well made, the life is well led;
and that when **Prayer** is discomposed,
the life groweth also into disorder. *Rectè nouit viuere, qui rectè nouit orare*, sayth
S. Augustine. He knoweth how to liue
well, who knoweth how to pray wel.

Aug. ho:
4. ex 150.
quæ eius
nomine
circumf.

And *S. Iohn Climacus* sayth, that a
seruant of God deliuered a memorable
speach to him ; and it was this. *By the
very beginning of the morning, I do already
know, what kind of dayes worke, it will be;
Giuing to vnderstand therby, that if he com-
plyed well with his Prayer, in the morning, all
the rest would succeed well; and so, that it
would fall contrarily out, if either he did not
comply with it at all, or els did it not so well,*
as he

Climacus.

as he could. And the fame rule holds, with all the reft of a mans life. Our felues do take daily experiment herof; fo that when we make our *Prayer* well, we go fo well in order, fo cheerfull, & fo full of good purpofes and defires, that it is to make one wonder ; and contrariwife, if we take no care of our *Prayer*, all the good which we had gotten, is in the way to be loft.

Bonauen.
de progref.
religionis.
ca. 7.

    S. *Bonauenture* fayth : *Sine iſto ſtudio, omnis religio eſt arida, imperfecta, & ad ruinā promptior.* By not reforting to Praier all goes backward , and by and by comes in tepidity ; and then by litle and litle , the foule begins to grow weake and to wither, and to loofe that vigor, and breath, which it had before . And then, I know not how , thofe holy purpofes and firſt thoughts , grow to vaniſh ; and then begin to awake, and reuiue all our paſſions . Soone after , will a man finde himfelfe , to become much inclined to vayne mirth , and to talking and laughing, and paſſing away tyme idly , and fuch other vanityes as thofe ; and that which is worſe, the appetite of vayne glory is reuiued ,

                                        and

and the appetite of ambition, & such
other things, as formerly seemed to
haue beene dead.

The Abbot *Nilus* sayth, That Praier
is to be the glasse of the religious man,
and in this glasse, are we to view and
reuiew our selues daily, & that at leasure, that so we may come to see and
know our faults, & to be remouing such
deformityes, as we shall discouer in our
selues, And in this glasse also, are we
to behold and consider, the vertues
which shine in Christ our Lord; to the
end that we may go adorning, & beau-
tifying our soules, by the contemplation therof.

The glorious *S. Francis* was wont
to say, *Gratia orationis, viro religioso maxi-*
mè desideranda est: nullus enim sine ea, in Dei
seruitio, fructus sperari potest. One of the
things, which the religious man were
to desyre most, is the grace or guift of
Prayer: forasmuch as without it, no
fruit or profit can be hoped for, and by
it we may hope for any thing. *S. Thomas*
of *Aquine*, amongst many other graue
sentences which are related as from his
mouth, in the history of his life, was
wont

Nilus.

Lib. 1. Com-
formit p.
1. hist. Mi-
ser. c. 7.

S. Tho. p.
hist. S. Do-
minici li.
3. ca. 37.

wont to ſay, *That a religious man, with-*
out Prayer, was like a ſouldier, ſent vnarmed
into a battayle.

Tho. de
Villa noua
ca. 13. vitæ
ſuæ.
Note.

That holy Archbiſhop of Valencia,
Thomas de Villanoua ſaid, that Prayer was
like naturall heate in a mans ſtomack,
without which it was impoſſible for
the naturall life to preſerue it ſelfe, or,
that meate ſhould do it any good ; but
with that, any meat is diſgeſted & con-
cocted well, and the man is well nou-
riſhed, and all the parts of the body are
ſupplyed with vertue and ſtrength, for
the performance of al their operations :
So, ſayth he, without Prayer, the ſpirituall life of man cannot be conſerued,
but with Prayer it may. For by *Prayer*
the ſoule is refreſhed, and the ſpirit gets
ſtrength, for all the Actions, and Obe-
diences which it is to performe ; and
againſt all troubles, and difficultyes
which it is to vndergoe. By the helpe
of *Prayer*, all theſe things grow to be
diſgeſted, and made paſſable, & prooue
good bloud for the ſoule.

Finally, if we make that vſe of
Prayer which we ought, we ſhall find
therein, full remedy of all our infirmi-
tyes

tyes, and meanes to conferue vs in *Re-*
ligion and vertue; for if perhaps you forget your felues in point of *Obedience*, &
obferuation of your *Rules*; if you begin
to take certaine little libertyes; if that
paſſiõ which you are moſt ſubiect to ,
ſhould reſume a litle life, & reflouriſh;
by laying hold vpõ the help *of Prayer*,
all theſe inconueniences, will with the
fauour of our Lord, be ſoone checked,
& ſtayed. And if by chance, you grow
negligent, euen in the vſe of *Prayer* it
felte, and ſhould confent to ſome tepi-
dityes therein ; yet, by meanes of the
felfe ſame *Prayer*, you are to procure the
remedy, and to returne into your ſelues. We are furniſhed by *Prayer*, againſt
all kind of inconueniences, yea and
euen againſt the defects of *Prayer* it
felfe. And therfore they do very well
compare *Prayer*, who ſay, *That it is as the*
hand to the body, which is both an inſtrument Note,
for the whole body, and for it ſelfe alſo. For
the hand laboureth, to the end that the
whole body, may be fuſteyned, & for
all things which are neceſſary eyther
to the body or the ſoule; and ſo it doth
alſo labour for it ſelfe. For if the *hand*
be

be fore, the *hand* cureth the hand; if the *hand* be fowle, it wasketh it; if it be cold, it warmeth it; in fine, the *hand* is fit for all things: and iust fo it is, in the cafe of *Prayer.*

CHAP. III.

That we are much bound to God, for hauing made that thinge fo eafy to vs, which on the one fide is fo Excellent *, and on the other fo* Neceffary.

IT is but reafon that we confider, & ponder here, the great, and finguler fauour which our Lord God hath done vs, in ordayning, that *Prayer,* being in it felfe a thing fo excellent, and fo high, and being yet fo very neceffary, forafmuch as concerneth vs; he hath yet withall, made it fo eafy, as to place it in the hand, or power of vs all; & we may vfe it, at all tymes, and in all places, if we be difpofed. *Apud me* *oratio, Deo vita mea:* Prayer is at hand with me; to the end I may make it to my God, who giues me life, fayth the Prophet *Dauid.* Thofe gates of the mercy of God, are neuer fhut, but they stand

Pf. 41.9.

ſtand open to all; and at all tymes, we
ſhall euer find him at leaſure, and deſirous to ſhew vs fauour, yea and euen
ſoliciting vs, to aske it of him.

It is an excellent conſideration,
which is vſually brought to this purpoſe. If Almighty God ſhould giue
leaue, for once only in the Moneth,
that all ſuch as would, might enter
into his preſence to ſpeake with him ;
and that then, he would giue them
glad and gratefull audience, & would
grant their ſuites : without doubt, it
ought to be highly eſteemed, ſince it
would be highly eſteemed if any temporall King ſhould offer it. But then
how much more is it fit, that we value
it, as we ought, comming from the
hand of God: eſpecially ſince he offieth
it, and inuiteth vs to it, not only for
once in the moneth, but for euery day,
yea and many tymes in the ſame day.
Veſpere, & mane, & meridie, narrabo, & an- **Pſal. 54.**
nunciabo, & exaudiet vocem meam , ſayth **18.**
the Prophet imbracing all tymes , by
this ſpeach of his. At night, in the morning, at mid-day, and in the euening, I
will relate, & repreſent my troubles &

B   my

my miseries to Almighty God: & I am
full of confidence, that wherfoeuer &
whenfoeuer I shall refort to him, he
will heare me, & do me fauour. God is
not weary to haue vs aske of him, as mē
vfe to be: becaufe he growes not poore
by giuing, as they vfe to do. For man
how much more he giueth to another,
fo much the leffe remaines to himfelfe,
fo that he takes from himfelfe, what he
giues to them, and he impouerifheth
himfelfe, afmuch as he enricheth them.

And from hence it is, that men grow
weary and difgufted, when they are
peftered with fuiters; and if they giue
twice, or thrice, with a good will, they
will yet be weary, againft the next
tyme, and eyther they giue no more,
or els they do it, in fuch a fafhion, as
that it may be the laft. But God as the
Ad Rom.
8. 12. Apoftle *S. Paul* fayth, *Est diues in omnes
qui inuocant illum :* he is infinitly rich, &
fince he growes not poore by giuing,
he is not difgufted & growes not weary in being afked, althogh all the world
in euery minut of time fhold be making
fuites. For he is rich towards all, & defires to inrich vs all, without leauing
to

to be as rich as he was before . And as his riches are infinite , fo alfo his mercy is infinite towards the redrefle of al the miferyes of vs all . And he defires, that we fhould beg often, and that we fhould euer be reforting to him.

It is reafon therefore , that we acknowledge, and fhew all gratitude, for fo great a benefit and fauour ; and that we ferue our felues well, of fuch a large and profitable leaue ; procuring to be very affiduous , in the vfe of *Prayer.* For, as *S. Augustine* fayth, vpon thefe words, *Beneditus Deus, qui nõ amouit orationem meam, & mifericordiam fuam à me* : you may hold for certaine, that if our Lord do not take the vfe of *Prayer* from you, as litle will he take from you his *Mercy.* To the end therefore, that our Lord may not deuide his *Mercy* from vs ; let vs procure that we neuer leaue the vfe of *Prayer* , nor deuide it from our felues .

Pf.65.20.

Сᴴᴬᴾ. IV.

Of two Kinds of Mentall Prayer.

Lᴇᴀᴠɪɴɢ a part *Vocall Prayer* , which is an *Exercife* fo holy, & fo

B 2 much

much frequented by the *Church of God*, I will now, only treat of that, which is *Mentall*, wherof *S. Paul* the Apoftle

1. *Cor.* 14. fpeakes, when he writes to the *Corin-thians*; *Orabo fpiritu, orabo & mente* ; *pfallã fpiritu, pfallam & mente.* I will pray, I will fing, and I will cry out, with my fpirit, and with my hart. Two Kinds there are of *Mentall Prayer.* The one is common, and plaine; the other is moft efpeciall, extraordinary, and of parti-culer priuiledge, with indeed may be faid rather to be receiued, the to be offe-red, or made ; for fo thofe anciēt Saints, who were well verfed in *Prayer*, did

Dionyf.l.
2.*de Diuin.*
nominib. vfe to expreffe themfelues. *S. Dionyfius* the *Areopagite*, fayth of his Maifter *Hie-rotheus, Quod erat patiens diuina:* Wherby he meant to fay, that he did not fo much operate, as receaue that, which was giuen him by Almighty God.

There is a very great difference , be-tweene thefe two kinds of *Prayer.* For the former, may be taught, in fome fort, by wordes; but we are not able to

Apo. 2.
17. teach the later, becaufe wordes are not able to declare it. *Quia nemo fcit, nifi qui accipit.* It is a kind of *hidden Manna*, wherof

wherof no body knoweth, what it is,
but he who taftes it. Yea, and euen he,
cannot declare how it is, neither doth
himfelfe vnderftand, how it growes.
Caſsian notes very well, and brings for
this purpoſe, a ſentence of *S. Antony* the
Abbot, which he calleth celeftiall, &
diuine; *Diuina, cæleſtis, & plusquā humana
ſententia : Non eſt perfecta oratio, in quaſe
Monachus, vel hoc ipſum quod orat, intel-
ligit.* It is no perfect *Prayer* (ſaith this
Saint) when one remembreth himſelf,
or vnderſtandeth exactly what he
prayeth. This high, and ſublime, rich
Kind of *Prayer*, doth not permit to him
who prayes, that he conſider then,
what he is performing : nor, that he
make reflection vpō what he is doing,
or (to ſpeake more properly) what he
is, not ſo much doing, as ſuffering.

*Caſsian.
collat. 9.
Abbatis
Iſaac. c. 3. N*

As heere below it happeneth many
tymes, that a man wilbe ſo abſorpt, &
inebriated (as it were) with a buſineſſe,
that he remembers not himſelfe, nor
conſiders, where he is; nor makes reflection vpon what he thinkes; nor ob-
ſerues, in what ſort he thinks it. And
iuft ſo, in this perfect Kind of *Prayer*, a

Note.

B 3   man

man is so taken, and absorpt in God,
that he remembers not himselfe, nor
knowes not how that is, nor by what
way it comes, nor by what way it
goes; nor cares he then, for any Inuen-
tions, nor Preambles, nor Points ; nor
considers he whether this, or that, be
fit to follow, in his *Prayer.* This arriued to the foresaid *S. Anthony,* by the relation of *Cassian,* who put himselfe to
Prayer in the euening, and continued
therein, till the Sunne, of the day following, strucke his eyes; and he com-
playned of that Sun, for rising so early,
and taking from him, that other light,
which our Lord, interiorly bestowed
vpon him.

Bern. in ser. in Dominicam infra octa. Epiphan.

S. *Bernard* sayth of this Kind of
Prayer: *Rara hora, & breuis mora.* This
hower comes but seldome, and when
it comes, the tyme seemes short, wherin it lasts. For how long soeuer it be, it
seemes to haue passed, assoone as a
breath of wind would do. *S. Augustine*
feeling this kind of *Prayer* in himselfe,

Aug. Confess. lib. 10. cap. 40.

sayth thus to God: *Aliquando intromittis
me in affectum, multum inusitatum, intror-
sus, ad nescio quam dulcedinem, quasi perficia-
tur*

tur in me, nescio quid erit, quod vita ista non erit. Sometimes thou drawest me, into an interior, & most vnusuall affection of mind; to a sweetnes which is beyōd all expression; and which, if it might be continued and perfected in me, I know not what that felicity might be, which would not be conteyned, in such a life as this.

In this most speciall kind of *Prayer,* and *Contemplation,* *S. Bernard* placeth three degrees. The first, he compareth to *Eating,* the second to *Drinking* (which is done with more facility & delight then *Eating,* for there is no trouble in the chewing) and the third, in being *Inebriated.* And he brings to this purpose, that of the Spouse in the *Canticles, Comedite amici, & bibite, & inebriamini charissimi.* He sayth first, come *Eate*; secondly, come and *Drinke*; and thirdly, come and *Inebriate* your selues, with this Loue. This last, is the most perfect; And this, is rather to *receaue*, then to *impart.* Somtimes the *Gardiner* drawes the water, out of the *Well*, by the strength of this armes; and sometymes, whilst he holds his hands, one by the

other

Note

Cant. 9f.

other, comes a *shower* frō heauen, which sincks into, and softens the earth;& the *Gardiner* hath then no more to do, but to let it come, and to addresse it to the roote of those trees, to th'end that they may bring forth fruite .

So it is, with these two Kinds of *Prayer*. For the one of them, is sought with industry , being yet assisted by Gods grace;but the other is ready made to the hand. In the first, thou goest labouring, and begging, and feeding vpon that very beggery. But the second, doth furnish thee , with a full table, which God himselfe, hath prepared for thee,to free thee from all hunger; a table,full of riches and abundance: *Introduxit me Rex in cellaria sua* , sayth the *Spouse*; And Isay the Prophet , sayth : *Lætificabo eos, in domo orationis meæ* : *I will recreate and regale them, in the house of my Prayer.*

Cant. 1.3.

*Isa.*56.7.

This Kind of *Prayer*, is a most particuler guift of God, which he bestoweth vpō whome it pleaseth him. Somtymes , in payment of those seruices, which they haue done him; and of the much, which they haue mortified thēselues,

selues, and suffered for his Ioue. And
sometymes agayne, without any relation to any precedent merits of theirs.
For, in fine, it is a most free, and liberall grace of his owne; and he commu-
nicates it, to whome he will, accor-
ding to that of the Gospell, *Non licet* **Matt. 20:**
mihi quod volo facere? Shall not I per- **15.**
haps, haue power to dispose of my
owne goods, as I list? But this Kind of
Prayer, is not a thing which we are
able to teach.

And so there are some Author s who
are reprehended, and euen prohibited,
because they would needs teach, that,
which could neither be taught, nor
learned ; and reduce that to Art, which
is aboue all art ; as if they could infal-
libly place a man in state of *Contempla-*
tion. Which *Gerson* doth well repre- **Gerson.**
hed, in a book which he wrote against
Rusbrokius, in these words: *Thou haste*
pluckt of the flower ,from the roote. For as
the flowers pluckt from the roote, and
carried in the hand, do quickly wither,
& loose their beauty; so do these things,
which God communicateth to the
foule, after an internall manner, in this
high

high and rich Kind of *Prayer.* For in procuring to draw them out of that place, and to declare them, and communicate them to others; they loose their lustre, and their splendor.

And this do they, who will needs declare and teach, that which cannot be declared, no nor so much as vnderstood. Those *Anagogies*, those *Transformations* of the Soule, that silence & annihilation, that vnion without *mediū,* that deepe bottome of *Taulerus* ; for what doth it serue to speake of these things; for if thou vnderstand them, I do not ; nor do I know, what thou wouldest say. Nay, in this case, we are taught, and that very well, that there is this difference, belonging to this diuine *Science,* from others ; That before we can attayne to other *Sciences,* we must first vnderstand the *Termes* ; but in this, thou shalt not vnderstand the *Termes*, till first, thou haue attayned to the *Sciēce.* In other *Sciences,* the *Theorick* doth precede the *Practicke*; but in this, the *Practick* must precede the *Theoricke.*

Nay I say moreouer, that not only this

this *Prayer* cannot be taught, or declared by words, but not so much as your selfe are to desire to rayse, or place your selfe in his kind of *Prayer*, vnlesse God himselfe, do raise you to it, and place you in it. For this would be a great presumption and pride; & you should so deserue, to loose euen that *Prayer*, which you haue already; & so remaine voide of all. *Introduxit me in cellam vinariam*, sayth the *Spouse* in the *Canticles.* That vocation of God, to draw the soule into his secret retiringplace, to treat so familiarly with it, and the bringing it, into his *Cellar of wyne*, so to satisfy it, and inebriate it with his loue, is a most particuler guifte of God. The *Spouse*, did not presume to enter; but her fellow *Spouse*, tooke her by the hand, and drew her in. That raising of ones selfe, to the *Kiße of his mouth*, is not a thing which thou canst, or oughtest pretend, vnlesse he raise thee vp; for it would be a great presumption.

And so we see, that the *Spouse*, aspireth not so high. She is more bashfull, & humble then so; but she beseecheth her

Cant. 2. 4.

her fellow *Spouse*, that he will vouchsafe to giue her such a *Kiße. Osculetur
me, osculo oris sui*. As if he had said(as *S.
Bernard* speaketh) I cannot by any
strength of myne owne, arriue to this
Loue, and to this *Vnion*, and to so high
Contemplation , if he vouchsafe not to
giue it. It is he, who by his goodnes&
most gracious liberality, must sublyme
vs, to this *Kiße of his mouth*, to this most
high *Prayer*, and *contemplation*, if he be
pleased, that we may haue it. This is
not any such thing, as that we may presume to teach it, nor wherein we may,
or ought to vndertake.

*Cant. 1.1.
Bern. ser.
52. ex par-
uis.*

Chap. V.

*How the holy Scripture doth declare to vs,
thefe two Kinds of* Prayer.

THESE two Kinds of *Prayer*, wherof we haue spoken, the Holy
Ghost doth admirably declare, in the
39. Chap. of *Ecclesiasticus*. He sayth
there, of the*Wiseman*, which the Church
interpreteth by the word *Iust: Cor suum
tradet ad vigilandum, diluculo ad Dominum
qui*

*Ecclesiast.
39.6.*

qui fecit illum , & in conspectu Altissimi de-
precabitur. He firſt placeth ordinary
Prayer,by ſaying that a man *riſeth early*
*in the morning,*which is a tyme much ce-
lebrated *in Holy Scripture ,* as being fit
for **Prayer.***Mane aſtabo tibi.Praueni in ma-*
turitate, & clamaui.Prauenerunt oculi mei
ad te diluculo,vt meditarer eloquia tua.Ad te
de luce vigilo. He ſayth , *ad vigilandum ;*
becauſe he goes to be attentiue, and
watchfull; not to ſleepe, or to make a
kind of a pillow of his **Prayer.** *Cor ſuum*
tradet ; He deliuereth his hart vp to
Prayer; He is not there, with his body
alone, hauing ſent his hart away, a-
bout other buſineſſe, which the *Saints*
do call, *Cordis ſomnolentia.* A drowſy &
dull hart , is a great impediment to
Prayer;for it diminiſheth that reuerece,
which is neceſſary for him, who treats
with God .

   Now what is that which cauſeth
this reuerence,in the iuſt perſon? *Ad Do-*
minum,qui fecit illum, & in conſpectu Altiſ-
ſimi deprecabitur. To conſider,that I am
in the preſence of God , and that I go
to treate with that ſublyme Maieſty;
this makes me remaine in **Prayer** , with
                   atten-

Pſa. 5. 5.
Pſa. 118.
147. 148.
Pſa. 62. 1.

attention and reuerence. Let vs now
obserue, what *Prayer* it is; which he
makes. *Aperiet os suum in oratione, & pro*
delictis suis deprecabitur. He will open
his mouth in *Prayer*, and will begin,
desiring God to pardon his sinnes; and
with being penitent, and confounded
for them. This is that *Prayer*, which we,
for our parts, are to make; To bewaile
out miseryes and sinnes, and to beg
Gods mercy, and pardon for them. We
must not content our selues to say, *I*
made a generall Confession of my life, at the
beginning of my conuersion, and then I enter-
tayned my selfe some dayes, in bewailing and
repenting my selfe of my sinnes: For no reason will permit, that we should forget
our sinnes, though we haue confessed
them; but we must still procure to carry them before our eyes, according to
that of the Prophet, *Et peccatum meum*
contra me est semper : and my sinne is euer
before me.

Psal. 50. 4.

     S. *Bernard*, vpon these wordes,
Lectulus noster floridus, sayth very well.
Your bed, which is your hart, is
still offensiue, and of ill sauour; for you
haue not yet taken vtterly away, the
                      ill

Bernard
ser. 46. su-
per Cant.
&. 55.

ill fmell of thofe vices, and vnmortifyed affections , which you brought
from the world. And will you then
prefume, to inuite the *Spoufe*, to repofe
in it? And dare you treate of other **Note.**
higher exercifes of *Loue*, and *vnion* with
Almighty God, as if you were already *Pfa.6.7.*
perfect? Deale firft, in clearing, and wa-
fhing well your bed with tears; *Lauabo*
per fingulos noctes lectum meam, lachrymis
meis ftratum meum rigabo; And then be
diligent, in adorning that bed of yours,
with the flowers of *vertues,* and fo you
may induce the *Spoufe* to come to it, as
the *Spoufe* in the *Canticles*, inuited hers.
Deale firft about the *Kiffe of his feete*, by
humbling your felfe, and by much
lamenting your finnes ; and then a-
bout a *Kiffe of his hands*, which is, by offering good workes to God, and by
procuring to receaue from his holy
hands, all true and folide vertue. And as
for that third *Kiffe of his mouth*, which is
that moft high *Vnion*, leaue that for fuch
tyme, as when our Lord fhall vouch-
fafe to raife you to it.

It is related of a very fpirituall *Fa-*
ther, that he remained twenty years, in
the

Doctour
Aracz.
the practife, and exercifes of the *Purgatiue way*; but we do inftantly growe
weary, & wilbe rifing vp in all haft,
to that *Kiffe of the mouth*, & to the Exercifes of the *Loue* of God. A body had
need of a deep foundation, for the rai-
fing of fo high a building. And moreouer, here is, in the *Exercifes* of the *Purgatiue way* (befides many other helpes &
benefits, wherof we fhall fpeake afterward) this one, of being a great reme-
Tract.8.c.
21.& p.2.
Tract.7.c.
4.
dy, and a medicine very preferuatiue,
againft falling into finne. For he who
goeth cötinually in actuall deteftation
of him, and in being wounded & confounded, for hauing offended Almighty God, in tyme paft; wilbe very far,
from committing new finnes in the
prefent tyme. And on the contrary
part, the *Saints* haue obferued, and de-
Note.
liuered vnto vs, that the caufe why
fome haue fallen, who feemed to haue
beene very fpirituall, & men of *Prayer*,
and peraduenture were fo indeed, hath
beene for want of this *Exercife:* and becaufe they gaue themfelues in fuch fort,
to others, and to certayne fweet and
guftfull confiderations, that they forgot

got the Exercise *of the knowledge of them-*
selues, and the confideration of their finnes, and fo they came to be to fecure, &
not to be fo wary, and timerous , as
they ought; and by thefe degres, they
came to fall. Becaufe they forgot fo
foone, their owne bafenefle, they fell
from that height, where they concey-
ued themfelues to be. It will therefore
be fit for vs, that our *Prayer* be imploied
for longe tyme, in the bewayling of
our finnes, as the *Wifeman* fayth; till   *Luc.* 14.
our Lord reach vs forth his hand, and   10.
fay to vs, *Amice, afcende fuperiùs.*

Let vs now caft an eye, to fee what
kind of thing, that high, and moft excellent *Prayer* is, which our Lord doth
giue, when he is pleafed. The *Wifeman*   *Ecci.* 39.
fayth prefently, *Si enim magnus Domi-*   8.
nus voluerit, fpiritu intelligentiæ replebit il-
lum. If he will (for this is no right of
inheritance, but a grace which is meer-
ly gracious, & of great liberality) thou
fhalt be fometymes in *Prayer*, & it wil
happen to thee, to haue a beame come
from heauen, and a flafh of lightning,
wherby thou art fhewed the way to
vnderftand things *truely*; & thou doeft
C   grow

grow to prize, and value that which
before thou dideſt not vnderſtād. This
is the guiſt of *Prayer*. How often had
you paſſed ſuch, or ſuch a Truth, and
neuer reflected vpon it, as then you
do. The holy Scripture calls it, *a Spirit
of Intelligence*, becauſe it ſeemeth to conſiſt, but of one *ſingle, and ſimple apprehen-
ſion*; ſo quiet, and ſetled is a man, with
ſuch a light as this. It happens to one
heere, as when he chaūceth vpon ſome
exquiſite, and curious Picture, to be
looking vpon it long togeather, without ſtirring ſo much as an eye, & without any diſcourſe of mind; but with a
guſte, with a ſuſpenſion, and with a
great admiration, and the eye is neuer
ſatisfyed with beholding it . Of this
ſort is this kind of *Prayer*, and this high
ſublime *Contemplation*. Or, to ſay better,
this *Contēplation*, hath ſomewhat of the
māner of that, which the glorious ſoules inioy in heauen, by *the viſion of God*.

The felicity of glorious ſoules, cō-
ſiſteth in the *Viſion* and *Contemplation* of
God; and in heauen we ſhalbe all abſorpt, and ouerflowed, by ſeeing, and
louing God, for all eternity, with one
ſimple

1900745

simple *Vision* of that Maiesty, enioying
his presence, and his glory without vse
of discourse, and without being euer
weary of beholding him . Nay for
euer, that *Song* of ours, and that diuine
Manna, willbe new vnto vs; and still
we shalbe taken, as it were, with new
admiration. In this very manner, is that
high and perfect *Prayer*, which is called *Contemplation*, whē our Lord is pleased to bestow it. For the man is neuer
satisfyed with beholding and contem-
plating God, & without any discourse
or wearinesse, but onely with one simple sight .

    The Scripture sayth, *Replebit illum,* *A poc.* 14.
becaufe this grace is fo copious, and fu- 3.
perabundant, that it ouerflowes, and
cannot be comprehended , in fuch a
fmall veffell. And it addeth inftantly ,
that which followeth vpon this, *Et ipfe* Note.
tanquam imbres, mittet eloquia fapientiæ fuæ;
& in oratione confitebitur Domino . From
hence grow inftantly, thofe *Colloquiums*
with God. This is the proper tyme,
for treating with his diuine Maiefty,
when the foule is moued, and inftructed, and fublymed , by that celeftiall
      C 2   light.

light, and wifdome. And fo B. *Fa. Ig-*
natius fayth, that this is the time, when
the *Colloquiums* are beft made, *Occurrente*
nobis fpirituali motu, ad Colloquia veniamus.
Let that word be well noted. When
firft we haue holpen our felues, by the
difcourfe of the powers of our mind, in
Meditation, and *confideration* of the *miftery;*
and when that *Meditation,* is growen
already to haue inflamed our hart; and
when we find our felues throughly
moued to it; then is the tyme of *Colle-*
quium, and of familiar treaty with Almighty God, and of our fuits, & nego-
tiatiõs with him. For the *Prayer* which
fpringeth from that hart, which already is touched by Almighty God, is
the *Prayer* which he heares ; and which
findes a good difpatch, at the hands of
his maiefty. For as *S. Auguftine* fayth,
When God moueth a man to aske any thing
of him, it is an euident figne, that he meanes
to grant that which is asked. This is that
moft excellent *Prayer,* which God giueth to whome he will. *Si enim Domi-*
nus magnus voluerit, fpiritu intelligentiæ re-
plebit illum. if our Lord, who is great, &
powerfull, will; we may eafily vfe this
high,

P. N. Ig-
natius lib.
Exercit.
fpirit. in
repetit. 1.
& 2 Exer-
cit. primæ
hebdoma-
dæ.

Aug. l. de
Verbis
Dom. fer.
&c. 82.

high , & aduantagious kind of Prayer.

But if our Lord will not be pleased, to raise vs vp to so high Prayer as
this, we must not (sayth *S . Bernard*) afflict our selues, or be dismaid ; but we
must be well contented to liue in the
exercise of vertue, and with the happi-
nesse of being conserued by our Lord,
in his friendship, and grace ; and in
that he suffer vs not, to fall into sinne.
*Vtinam detur mihi pax, bonitas, gaudium in
spiritu Sancto; misereri in hilaritate; tribuere
in simplicitate; gaudere cum gaudentibus; flere
cum flentibus, & his contentus ero.* I would
to God, our Lord were pleased to giue
me peace , goodnes, ioy in the holy
Ghost; mercy, simplicity , and charity
with my neighbours, for with this
would I content my selfe. *Cætera san-
ctis Apostolis , virisq; Apostolicis derelinquo.*
Those other high Contemplations, I
leaue to the Apostles and Apostolicall
men : *Montes excelsi ceruis, petra refugium
herinacijs.* Those high mountaines of
contemplatiõ , let them be for such as
do, with the swiftnesse of Harts and
Roes, runne at full speede to perfection ; I , who am no better then a

meere

Notes.

*Bern. ser;
46.super
Cant.*

Ps.103. 18.

*1 Cor.12.
4.*

meere hedg-hog, full of faults and sinnes,
will betake my selfe to the holes, and
concauities of that *Rocke*, which is
Christ our Lord; to hide my selfe in his
wounds, and to wash away my faults,
and sinnes, with the bloude which
floweth out from thence; and this
shalbe my kind of *Prayer*.

But now, if the glorious *S. Bernard*
content himselfe with the only exercise of vertue, and with griefe & contrition for sinne, and do leaue this other
most excellent *Prayer* for Apostolicall
mē, & for those great *Saints*, to whome
our Lord is pleased to communicate
the same; it wilbe agreable to all reason, that we also be content therewith;
and that this be our exercise in *Prayer*,
to be wounded with griefe, and confounded with the shame of our sinnes;
and to attend to the mortification of
our passions; and to the rooting vp of
vice, and vicious inclinations; and to
ouercome all repugnances, & difficultyes, which may offer themselues to
vs, as impediments in the way of vertue. And as for that other most excellent, and most aduantagious kind of
Prayer,

Prayer, let vs leaue it, till such tyme as our Lord may be pleased to call, and raise vs to it.

Yea, and also euen then, when we conceiue our selues to be called to it, we had need to very cautelous, & well aduised; for in this there hath beene much abuse, and errour. Sometimes a man will thinke that God doth call him to this *Prayer*, by, I know not what kind of delight, and sweetnes, or facility, which he findes in the exercise of *the loue of God*; whereas indeed, God doth not call him to it; but it is the man himselfe, who mounts, and will needs intrude himselfe, because the diuell deceaues, & blindes him, to the end that he may leaue the desire of obtayning that, whereof he hath most need, and so, vpon the whole matter, he may do nothing, and neither profit in the one, nor other kind. There is a great maister of spirit, who sayth thus very well. As a Man would shewe « himselfe to be of little wisdome, if he, « whome the King had commaunded to « assist and serue him at his table, should « presumptuously sit downe at the same «

Note.

Blosius in speculo spirit. cap. XI.

C 4 table,

» table, without the commaundment, or
» so much as leaue of the King; so doth
» he very ill, and indiscreetly, who deli-
» uereth himselfe all ouer, to the sweete
» & delightfull rest of *Contemplation*, not
» being euidently called to the same, by
» God himselfe. And *S. Bonauenture*, doth
herein giue an excellent good aduice,
and sayth : Let a man exercise himselfe
in that which is profitable and secure;
which is, in extirpating of vices, and ill
dispositions, and in acquiring true and
solide vertue. For this is a very playne
and safe way, wherein there can be no
deceit; but so much the more, as one
shall endeauour to perfect himselfe in
mortification, humiliation, and resignation, so much the more shall he
please God, and deserue more in his
sight. And as for these other exquisite
and extraordinary wayes, there are
(saith *S. Bonauenture*) may errours committed, and many illusions of the diuell imbraced by occasion thereof. For,
many tymes, one thinks, that, to be of
God, which is not of God; and that, to
be some great matter, which is nothing;
and therefore these latter, are to be examined

Bonauent.
de processu
religionis.
c. 20.

mined by thofe former ; and not thofe,
by thefe. This is the generall doctrine
of the *Saints*, as fhortly we fhall fee.

CHAP. VI.

*In which the fame doctrine, is more de-
clared and confirmed.*

FOR the better declaration, & confirmation of this Doctrine , the
Saints, and Maifters of fpirituall life do
heere obferue, That for the obtayning
of this *Prayer*, and high *Contemplation*,
wherof we haue fpoken, there is need
of great mortification of our paffions;
and that a man be very well grounded
in the mortal vertues; and that he exercife himfelfe long in them; & if not,
they fay it is in vayne , for a man to
pretend to enter into *Contemplation*, &
to make profeffion therof. *Oportet* (fay
they) *vt priùs fis Iacob luctans , quam Ifrael
Deum videns, ac dicens, Vidi Deum facie ad
faciam. It will firft, be neceffary, that thou be
a ftrong, and ftoute wraftler , and that thou
ouercome thy paffions, and peruerfe inclinations if thou defire to arriue to that intimate
ynion, with Almighty God. Blofius fayth,*
that

*Greg. li. 7.
mor. c. 27.
Bern. fer.
46. fuprà
Cant. Ifi-
dor. li. 3. ca.
25.
S. Tho. q.
184. art. 3.
& Caiet,
in Gen.
32. 30.*

Blosius in tabula spi-rituali. ad-dit. 1.

that he who pretends to arriue to some very eminent degree of diuine loue, & yet procureth not, with great diligence, to correct and mortifie his vices, and to driue from himselfe, all inordinate loue of creatures, is like a man, who being loaden with leade, & iron, and withall being bound, hand, and foote, will yet needs clyme vp, to some very high tree.

And therefore they aduise such as are *Maisters* in matter of *spirit*, that before they treate of *Contemplation* with them whome they instruct, they must treate of the way, how to mortify all their passions very well; and how to acquire the habits of Vertue, of Patience, of Humility, of Obedience; and that they exercise themselues much herein. This they call the *Actiue Life*, which must go before the *Contemplatiue.* And for want of this methode, many, who would not walke by these steps, but would needs peruert the order, and clyme vp easily to *Contemplation*, do find themselues, after many years of *Prayer*, to be very voide of *vertue*, and to be *impatient, harsh*, and

proude;

proude; and that if you touch them a little in this Kind , they are ready, through impatience, to breake out into paffionate words, wherby they well difcouer their imperfection & immortification.

This is very well declared by our Father *Generall*, *Euerardus Mercurianus*, in a letter which he wrote about this fubiect, in thefe words: Many who did more want difcretion, then abound with true defire of proceeding, in the way of fpirit, hauing heard that there is another more high exercife of *Prayer*, of *the loue of God*, of certaine *Anagogicall Acts*, and of I knowe not what kind of *Silence*; would needs mount vp to the Exercife of the vnitiue way, before their ryme; hauing heard men fay, that this Exercife was more heroicall and perfect; and that Vice , is better ouercome therby, and Vertue alfo obteyned more eafily , and more fweetely. And becaufe they rofe to this , before their time, they loft much time; and made no way; and at the end of many yeares, they found themfelues as quick in their paffions, and vnchanged in their

Euerardus Mercurianus.

C 6

their ill affections; & as great friends of
delight, and eafe , as if they had neuer
entred into any conuerfation, or communication with almighty God. And
they haue beene as ftiffe, in purfuite of
their owne will, and as hardly haue
beene drawne, to fubmit their iudgment, when their Superiors were min-
ded to difpofe of them, contrary to
their owne liking and dictamen , as if
it had beene the firft day. And the reafon of this is, becaufe they would needs
fly, before they had wings ; and they
would needs find out certaine neere
ways, and would not walke by the
fteps which they were to tread . They
would not ground themfelues firft, in
mortification , nor in the practife of
vertue; and fo it is no maruell, if without a foundation , they could not raife
a good houfe. They built vpon fand,
and fo they haue failed , when there
was moft need.

To the end that it may appeare,
how true, and vniuerfall this doctrine
is, you fhall vnderftãd, that this which
here I haue deliuered, is vfually taught
by holy writers, when they fpeake of
three

three parts, or three kindes of *Prayer*, according to those three Wayes, which they call *Purgatiue, Illuminatiue, & Vnitiue.* Which is a doctrine, drawne out of *Dionysius* the *Areopagite*; & from him it was taken by *S. Gregory Nazianzen.* and by all the rest of them, who haue treated of spirituall matters. They say, and they all agree in this, That before there be any treating of this high, and most complete kind of *Prayer*, which carrieth correspondence with the *Vnitiue Way*, we are euer to handle that, which belongeth to the *Purgatiue*, & *Illuminatiue Way.* It is necessary for vs first, to exercise our selues in griefe, & repentance for our sinnes; and in rooting vp our vices, & ill affections; & in acquiring of true *Vertues*, by imitating Christ our Lord, in whom they shine. If we should passe forward, without this, we should go on, without a ground, and so at last, we should faile, like him who would needs passe vp to the highest *Classe* in learning, without hauing grounded himselfe in the lowest; or who would clyme as high as the last step of the ladder, without tou-

Diony-
sius A-
reopagi-
ta.
Gregory
Nazian-
zen.

touching vpon the firſt.

CHAP. VII.

Of the ordinary Kind of Mentall Prayer.

LAYING aſide, that particuler, and extraordinary Kind of *Prayer*, ſince we cannot teach it, nor declare what it is, nor in what manner it growes, neither is it in our power to compaſſe it; nor doth God command vs to attaine it; nor ſhall we yeild any accompte to him, for the want ther-of: we will now fall to treate of that ordinary kind of *Mentall Prayer*, which may, in ſome ſort, be taught, and obtey-ned by indeauour, and aduiſe, being firſt aſſiſted therein, by the grace of our Lord.

Amongſt other fauours, and bene-fits which our Lord hath done to the *Society*, this hath beene a very great one, that he hath giuen vs, the kind of *Prayer*, which we are to hold, appro-ued by the *Sea Apoſtolicke*, in that

booke

booke of the *Spirituall Exercises*, composed by our *B. F. Ignatius*, as appeares
by that *Breue*, which is placed in the
beginning of the said booke. Wherein
Pope Paul the third (after he had caused
them to be examined, with great ex-
actnesse) doth approue and confirme
them; declaring them to be very profitable, and vsefull; and he much exhor-
teth all faythfull Christians to exercise themselues therein.

　Our Lord God, did communicate
this Kind of Prayer to our *B*. *Father* ,
and he communicated the same to
vs, who are of the same *Order*, which
our Lord had communicated to him.
And so we are, to haue greate confidence in God , that by this way and
meanes , which he hath found out
for vs, he will help vs , and do vs fauour ; since herby , he gayned our *B*.
Father, and his companions ; and since
that tyme , many others. And there,
did our Lord communicate, the way
and trace of the *Society*, to our *B*. *Father*, as himselfe said; and we are not to
seeke out other ways of *Prayer*, which
are extraordinary ; but to procure to
mould

Libro de
los Exer-
citios espi-
ritua es de
N. B. P.
Ignatio
approba-
do.

mould our felues, according to that forme, which we haue, from him, like vnto his true, and lawfull Children.

Note,

In this Exercife *of the three Powers*, which is the firft of the Exercife; our *B. Father* doth teach the manner, which is to be held in *Prayer*, throughout all the reft of the *Exercifes.* And it is, that whatfoeuer point we fhall take in hand, we muft go exercifing the *three powers of our foule*, the *Memory*, the *Vnderftanding*, and the *Will.* The memory, is firft to place before the eyes of our *vnderftanding*, that *point*, or *myftery*, vpon which we meane to *pray.* Then we enter with our *vnderftanding*, difcourfing, meditating, & confidering thofe things, which may helpe vs moft, towards the mouing of our *Will*; & then laftly the affections of the fame *Will*, muft follow. Now this *third*, is the principall thing, wherupon we are to ftay. For this, is the end of the *Meditation*, and the *Fruite*, which muft be drawen, out of all thofe confiderations, and difcourfes of the *Vnderftanding*. All I this fay muft be ordained, to

move

moue the *Will*, to a desire of that which
is good, & a detestation of that which
is bad. And therfore, is the name of
the three Powers, giuen to this first *Exercise*, because it is the first, wherein this
manner of *Prayer* is taught; for otherwise, these *three Powers of the soule*, are
to be imployed in all the other *Exercises* following, as well as in this.

This kind of *Prayer*, which here
our *B. Father* teacheth, and which the
Society vseth, is not subiect to any sin-
gularity, nor hath it any thing in it,
which may carry any proportion to
illusions, as some others haue. But it
is a Kind, which is very playne, and
much vsed by the ancient Fathers, &
very conforme to mans nature, which
is discursiue, and rationall, and which
gouernes it selfe by reason; and is per-
swaded, conuinced, and subdued by it,
and consequently it is most easy, most
fruitfull, and most safe. So that we are
not to remaine in our *Prayer*, like persons who had giuen ouer our selues;
or as if we were extraordinarily illu-
minated, without doing any thing on
our part, for this would be a great

D   errour

errour and abuse : But we are to call
vpon God, by meanes of the *Exercise
of our powers,* and we are gently, to coo-
perate with him ; because God is pleased, to require the cooperation of his
creatures ; & this is that, which our *B.
Father* teacheth vs, in his booke of the
spirituall Exercises.

Those other kinds of *Prayer,* which
take away all discourse, and which vse
certaine *negations,* with certaine *silen-
ces,* and are taken out of *Mysticall Theology,* are not vsually to be taught, no
nor so much as to be sought, as was
said before. And new beginners who
haue not proceeded far, in the knowledge of their *Passions,* and in the practise of *Vertue* , being directed into
these particuler ways, are made subiect to illusions, and deceytes. And
when they thinke they haue gayned
much vpon themselues , they find by
experience, that all their passions remaine entire, which by meanes of that
sweet bayte, and guste of *Prayer* , lay
a while, as if they had beene asleepe,
but afterward they awake, with much
danger to the owners. Besides, that

*Cap. 4. &
5.*

by

by thefe particuler, and fingular kindes of *Prayer*, there is created in men,
a kind of ftiffnes , and clofnes to their
owne Iudgment, which is a great dif-
pofition , towards a mans being de-
ceiued. And therefore our B. F. *Ignatius*, did apprehend it much; and he
faid, that ordinarily, fuch perfons haue
a touch of this.

I fay therefore, that the *firſt thing*
which we are to do in *Prayer*, in any
Pointe which we fhall take in hand,
muft be to place, before our *memory*,
that *point*, or *myſtery*, vpon which we
meane to make our *Prayer*; then we
muft enter into *Meditation*, by difcourfing with the *Vnderſtanding* , vpon the
particularityes of that *myſtery*, & then
come in, the affects of the *Will*. So that
the Memory firft propounds, & then
inftantly enters Difcourfe, and *Meditation* of the *Vnderſtanding*; for this is the
ground, from whence all thofe acts &
Exercifes, are to flowe, which we produce in *Prayer* ; and in the vertue and
ftrength of this , all the reft is performed .

Now the reafon of this is cleere, in

good *Philosophy*. For our *Will* is a blind
kind of *Power*, which cannot ſtir a
foote, vnleſſe it be guided by the *Vnderſtanding. Nihil volitum, niſi pracogni-
tum.* This is a common maxime of the
Philoſophers, The *Will* cannot deſire
that thing, which hath not already
paſſed by the *Vnderſtanding ;* which is as
the *Page* with a torch in his hand, who
goes before, to giue light to the *Will, &*
guides it, and diſcouereth to it, what
it is to *loue,* or what to hate. And ſo *S.
Auguſtine* ſayth, *Inuiſa diligi poſſe, incog-
nita nequaquam.* And *S. Gregory* ſayth:
Nemo poteſt diligere, quod prorſus ignorat.
Well may we *loue* the thing we haue
not *ſeene,* but that wherof we haue
no *Knowledge,* we cannot *loue ;* For the
obiect of our *Will,* is *ſome Good apprehen-
ded,* or *vnderſtood.* For therfore, do we
like, or *loue* any thing, becauſe *we ap-
prehēd it as good,* & worthy to be loued;
and on the other ſide, we do therfore
abhor, and fly from any thing, as iud-
ging and apprehending it to be ill, &
worthy to be abhorred. And ſo, when
we deſire, that any man ſhould change his will, and purpoſe, we perſwade
him

Note.

Aug. li.
10. de Tri.
c. 1.
Greg. ho.
36. ſuper
Euangel.

him with reafon, and we procure to
conuince his *Vnderftanding*, that the
thing which he defires, is not conuenient, nor good; and that the other
thing is better, and more conuenient;
that fo he may forfake the one, and
imbrace the other. So that the act, &
difcourfe of the *Vnderftanding*, is the
foundation & ground, of thofe other
acts, and *Exercifes*, which we make in
Prayer; and therfore is *Meditation* fo neceffary. Which point we will declare
yet further, in the Chapters following.

Chap. VIII.

Of the neceffity of Meditation.

HVgo of *S. Victor* fayth, that
Prayer cannot be perfect, if *Medi-*
tation do not eyther go before it, or
with it. And this is alfo the doctrine
of *S. Auguftine*, who fayth, That *Prayer*
without Meditation, is but a tepide
kind of thing. This they proue very
well; for if a man do not exercife himfelfe in knowing, and confidering his
mifery, and weakeneffe, he will go in
errour,

*Hugo de
Sancto
Vict. tra.
de laude
orationis,*

Auguftin.

D 3

errour, and will not be able to aske in
Prayer, that which is fittest for him, &
when he asketh, it will not be with
such feruour, as were conuenient.
There are many, who, by reason that
they know not themselues, & confider not their faults, do go on, in the
wrong way, and do presume of themselues in certaine things, which they
would not do, if they knew themselues; & so they treate in their *Prayer*,
about certaine things, which are very
different from those, wherof they haue
most need. If therfore you will know
how to pray, and to beg of God, what
is fit for you, see you exercise your felues, in the consideratio of your owne
faults, & frailtyes. And by this meanes
you shall know what to aske; and by
vnderstanding, and considering your
great necessity, you will aske it with
feruour, and as you ought, as poore
needy beggers vse to do, who well
know, and feele their necessity and
misery.

*Bern. ser. 1.
de sancto
Andrea.*   S. *Bernard*, (treating thus, that we
are not to go flying, but walking towards perfection, *Nemo repentè fit sum-*
                                mus;

mus; afcendendon on volando, apprehenditur summitas scale,) fayth, That we walking, and rifing towards perfection, are to be vpon thefe two feete, *Meditation* and *Prayer. Afcendamus igitur, velut duobus quibufdam pedibus, Meditatione & Oratione; Meditatio fiquidem docet, quid defit; Oratio, ne defit, obtinet.* For meditation points vs to what we want, and Prayer preuailes to obteyne it; *Illa viam oftendit, ifta deducit.* Meditation fhowes vs the way, and Prayer guides vs in it. *Meditatione denique, agnofcimus imminentia nobis pericula, oratione euadimus.* Finally, by meditation we know the daungers which threaten vs, and by Prayer we efcape and free our felues. From hence it is, that *S. Auguftine* fayth, that Meditation is the beginning of all good. *Intellectus cogitabundus, eft principium omnis boni.* For he who confiders how good God is in himfelfe; and how good & mercifull he hath beene to vs; how much he hath loued vs; how much he hath done, and how much he hath fuffered for vs; will quickly enkindle himfelfe, in the loue of fo good a Lord. And he that confiders well,

Auguftin.

Note.

D 4   his

his owne faults, & miseries, will soone
growe humble, and hold himselfe, in
small accompt. And he that considers, how ill he hath serued God, and
how grieuously he hath offended him;
will esteeme himselfe worthy of the
greatest punishment. And thus, by *Meditation*, we grow to enrich our soules,
with all vertue.

For this cause, doth the holy Scripture
recommend *Meditation* so much to vs.
*Blessed is the man, who meditates day and
night, in the law of our Lord*, sayth the
Prophet *Dauid. Et erit tanquam lignum,
quod plantatum est secus decursus aquarum,
quod fructum suum dabit in tempore suo*.
Such a man as this, is like a tree, planted neere to the streames of water,
which will giue much fruite. *Beati qui
scrutantur testimonia eius, in toto corde ex-
quirunt eum*. These are the men, who
seeke God with their whole hart ; and
this is that, which makes them seeke
him. And this is also that, which the
Prophet begged of God, towardes the
keeping of his law, *Da mihi intellectũ &
scrutabor legem tuam, & custodiam illam in
toto corde meo*. And on the contrary side,

Psa. 1. 3.

Psa. 118. 2.

*Psa. 118.
34.*

he

he fayth. *Niſi quod lex tua meditatio mea* *Pſa.118.*
eſt , tunc fortè peryſſem in humilitate mea. *92.*
If it had not been, that my vſuall meditation was vpon the law , perhaps
I had periſhed in my humility; that is *Hierome.*
in my *difficulties* , as *S. Hierome* ſhewes.
And ſo one of the greateſt prayſes ,
which the Saints aſcribe to *Meditation*,
and Conſideration, or rather the greateſt of them all, is this, That it is a
great helper on to all vertue. *Soror le-*
ctionis, nutrix orationis, directrix operis, om- *Gerſon.*
niumą; pariter perfectio, & conſummatrix
exiſtens.

By one contrary, a man comes to
know the other,beſt. One of the principall cauſes , of all thoſe miſchiefs
which are in the world, is want of
Conſideration , according to that of the
Propher *Ieremias, Deſolatione deſolata eſt* *Iere.12.11.*
omnis terra, quia nullus eſt qui recogitat cor-
de. The cauſe why the whole earth is
in ſuch ſpirituall deſolation, and that
there are in it,ſo many ſinns,is becauſe
there is ſcarce any one ,who entreth
into himſelfe , and maketh it his buſines to meditate, and reuolue the my-
ſteries of God, in his hart. For who is
he

he that would presume to commit a
mortall him, if he considered that God
died for sinne? And that it is so great an
euill, as that it was necessary that God,
should become man, to the end, that
he might satisfy for it, according to the
rigor of Iustice? Who would presume
to sinne, if he considered that for one
mortall sinne, God punisheth a man
with Hell-fire, and that for euer? If
men would put themselues to thinke,
and to ponder well that worde, *Disce-*
dite à me, maledicti, in ignem æternum, that
same *Eternity*, that *foreuer, without all end*;
and that *as long as God shalbe God , he is*
to burne in the fire of Hell , what man is
that, who in exchange of a momen-
tary delighte, would make choice to
imbrace such eternall torment?

S. Thomas of Aquine, was wont to
say, that it was past his vnderstanding,
how it was possible, that a man liuing in mortall sinne, could tell how
to laugh, or take any contentment.
And he had great reason to say so. For
that sinner, knowes for certayne, both
that if he should then dy, he should go
instantly, and for euer remaine in Hell;

Mat.25.41

In hist. Or-
din. S. Do-
minici. p.
1. li.3.c.
37.

Note.

and

and withall, that he hath not any se-
curity of continuing in his life, one
moment. There was one who had en-
tertained himselfe in banquets, and in
choice musicke, and in all kinde of
ioylity; but because a naked sword was
placed ouer his head, hanging vp, but
by a single thred, he grew all into
trembling for feare, of whé the sword
might fall; & nothing could giue him
guste. What then shall become of him,
who is threatned, not only with temporall, but eternall death, which dependeth vpon a little-little thred of
life? Since a man dyes suddenly sometymes, & at an instant; & he goes well
to bed, and the first tyme he awakes,
is to see himselfe in the flames of hell.

A good seruant of God, was wont
to say to this purpose, That in his opinion, there were to be but two kindes of prisons, in any Christian Common wealth. The one of the *Inquisi-*
tion, the other for *Mad-men.* For eyther
a man belieues, that there is a *Hell,*
made for such as sin, or no. If he belieue not this, let him be caried to the
Inquisition, for an *Hereticke.* If he belieue
it,

Damocles
apud Ci-
cer. Tusc.
5,

Note.

it, and yet neuerthelesse will remaine
in mortall sinne; let him be carried to
the house of *Mad-men*; for what greater madnesse can there be, then this?

There is no doubt, but that if se-
rioufly men confidered this, it would
be a ftrong bridle to reftrayne them
from sinne. And for the fame reafon,
doth the diuell procure, with so much
diligence, to hinder vs from this *Confi-*
deration, and *Meditation*. The firft thing
Iud.16. 21. that the *Philiftines* did to *Sampfon*, when
they had taken him, was to pluck out
his eyes; and so, this is the firft thing
which the diuell procures to do, to a
sinner. Since he cannot take his *Fayth*
from him, he procures that he may belieue, as if he belieued not. *Vt videntes*
Matt.13. *non videant, & audientes non audiant, neque*
13. *intelligant.* He procures that a man may
not confider that, which he belieues,
nor reflect vpon it, any more then if
he belieue it not. He bindes vp his
eyes; whic . . es to the fame reckoning for him, as if he were blind. For
as it serues to no purpose for a man to
open his eyes when he is in the darke,
becaufe he fhalbe able to see nothing;

so

fo (as *S. Augustine* fayth) it will profit
thee nothing, to be in the light, if thine
eyes be fhut; for fuch a one will fee as
little, as that other. For this it is, that
Meditation, and *Mentall Prayer*, is of fo
much importance, becaufe it opens our
eyes.

Aug. in
Pfal. 15.
prope fi-
nem.

CHAP. IX.

Of the great Benefit and Profit, which we are
to draw from Meditation; *and how we*
are to vfe it, to the end to profit by it.

IT will be of great profit to vs, that
in tyme of *Prayer*, we exercife our
felues, in the affects and defires of our
Will, of which part we fhall fhortly
treat. But it is very needfull withall,
that thefe affects and defires, go very
well grounded in reafon, and in truth;
becaufe man is a rationall creature, and
wilbe guided by reafon, & by the way
of *Vnderftanding*. And therefore, one of
the principall things, to which we
muft ordayne, and addreffe *Meditation*,
muft be, that we may remaine very
foundly *vnbeguiled*, and fully poffeffed,
with the knowledge of thofe things,
which

Note.

which are really true; and perfectly
conuinced, and refolued, concerning
what is beft for vs. We vfe to fay, when
one is reduced to leade an orderly and
good life, that he is *vnbeguiled*. This *vnbeguiling*, is therefore to be one of the
principall fruites, which we muft procure to gather from *Prayer*. And this
point, muft be much noted, becaufe it
is of very great importance, in this
matter. And efpecially, in the beginning of a fpirituall life, it is neceffary
that a man exercife himfelfe much
in this; to the end that he may go on,
well grounded, and poffeffed, with a
firme beliefe of things, which really
are true.

To the end, that we may better
draw this benefit from *Meditation*, and
that it may be of much profit to vs, it
wilbe neceffary that it be not fuperficially, nor curforily made; nor yet after a dull, and dead fafhion; but with
life, and with much attention, and reft
of mind. You are to *Meditate*, & confider at large, and with great quietnes,
the fhortnes and frailty of this life; the
vanity of the things of this world; &
                                        how

how the arriuall of death, makes an
end of them all; that so you may despise all worldly things, and place your
whole harte, vpon that which is to
last for euer. You are to consider, and
ponder often, what a vaine, and idle
thing, the estimation and opinion of
men is, which maketh such fierce war
vpon vs. For it neither giues any thing
to you, nor takes any thing from you,
nor can it make you, a whit better, or
worse. Grow you thus to despise it, &
make no reckoning at all therof. And
the same, is to be done in the rest. And
by this meanes, a man goes *Vnbeguiling*
himselfe, by little and little; and to be
conuinced, and resolued vpon that
which is for his good; & he groweth
thus to become a spirituall man. *Sedebit* *Threu.3.*
solitarius, & tacebit; quia leuauit se super se. 28.
He goeth lifting himselfe aboue him-
selfe; and is procuring to haue a hart
truly generous, which despiseth all
things of this world; and he growes
to say with *S. Paul,* *Propter quem, om-*
nia detrimentum feci, & arbitror vt stercora,
vt Christum lucrifaciam. That which be- *Phil.3.8.*
fore I held for gaine, I now hold for
                                        losse;

loffe; yea and euen for dung, that I may gaine Chrift our Lord.

There is a great deale of difference betweene *Meditating* and *Meditating*, & betweene *knowing* and *knowing*. For the wife man, knoweth a thing after one fafhion; and the fimple and ignorant man, after another. The wife man knoweth it, as it is indeed; but the fimple man knoweth only the exterior, and apparence thereof. If an ignorant perfon find a pretious ftone, he likes it for the fplendor, and exterior beauty therof, and for nothing els, becaufe he knoweth not the value of it. But the wife *Lapidary*, when he meeteth with fuch a one, he defires it much; not only for the fplendor, and exterior beauty, but becaufe he well vnderftandeth the value, and vertue therof. Now this is the very difference; betweene him who knowes how to *Meditate*, & confider fpirituall things, and diuine myfteries; and him who knowes it not. For this later kinde of man, doth but looke vpon things fuperficially, and as it were vpon the skinne; and although he like them well, for the luftre and fplen-

Note.

fplendor, which he difcerneth there,
yet he is not much taken, with a true
defire therof. Wheras he who knoweth how *to Meditate*, and ponder thofe
things well, growes *vnbeguiled*, and
well refolued. For knowing the true
value of the *treafure* which is hidden,
and of this *pretious pearle*, which at the
laft, he hath found; he defpifeth all
the reft, in comparifon therof. *Abijt, &* *Matt. 13.*
vendidit omnia, quæ habuit, & emit eam. *46.*

This difference, doth Chrift our
Lord declare to vs, in the holy *Gofpell*,
in the hiftory of that *woman*, who was
fubiect *to a bloudy fluxe.* The holy Euan- *Matt. 9.*
gelifts do relate, how the Redemer of *20.*
the world, going to reuiue, and recouer that Daughter of the *Prince of the*
Sinagogue, there went fo much people, *Luc. 8. 43.*
as to make a preffe about him. A cer-
taine woman fawe him paffe, who
had beene fubiect *to a bloudy fluxe twelue*
years, and fhe had wafted all her goods
vpon *Phifitians*, and gotten no health,
in exchange, but rather grewe worfe
and worfe. And with a defire which
fhe had, to recouer health, fhe brake
through the middeft of that people, &

E   with

with great confidence, and fayth, said within herselfe; *Si tetigero tantùm vesti- mentum eius, salua ero.* If I can but touch the skirt of his garment, I am safe. She approacheth, she toucheth, & instant- ly that spring of bloud was dryed vp. Christ our Lord, lookes backe, and sayth, *Quis me tetigit?* *Who is that, which hath touched me?* S. *Peter*, and the rest of the disciples, answered; *Praeceptor, turbae te comprimunt, & affligunt, & dicis, quis me tetigit?* Maister the troopes presse vpon you, and do you say, who hath touched me? *Tetigit me aliquis, nam & ego noui, vir- tutem de me exijsse.* I meane not so, sayth Christ our Lord; but I meane, that some body hath touched me, not after the fashion of other folkes, but in a more particuler manner; *For I find that Vertue is gone out of me.*

Yea, that indeed was the businesse; this was indeed, to touch Christ our Lord; and this is that, of which he as- ked. For as for the other kind of tou- ching by chance, and in that vulgar manner, there is no great account to be made therof. Heere then consists, all the substance of the matter, *in touching*

Christ

Chrift our Lord, and his holy myfteries, in fuch forte, as that we may feele the fruite, and vertue of it, in our felues. And for this purpofe, it importeth much, that we go to our *Meditation* with attention; and that we ruminate, and take things in funder, at good lea-fure. The meat with is not chewed, is neither bitter nor fweet, and therfore the ficke man fwallowes the Pills downe whole, to the end that they may not be offenfiue to him. And for the felfe fame-reafon, doth not *finne,* nor *death,* nor the *laft Iudgment,* nor the eternall *torments of Hell,* feeme bitter in the mouthe of a finner, becaufe he cheweth not thefe things; but he fwal-lowes them whole, and takes them vpon truft, and in groffe, as they come. And for the felfe fame reafon alfo, doth the *miftery* of the *incarnation, pafsion,* and *refurrection* of Chrift our Lord, and the reft of the benefits of Almighty God, giue to many, little delight, or guft; becaufe they do not chew, nor rumi-nate, nor ponder thefe things as they ought. Do you but fhew, and breake this graine of muftardfeed, & pepper,

and

and you shall quickly see, how it will bite, and fetch the teares from your eyes.

Chap. X.

Of other benefits, and profits which there are, in the vse of Meditation.

S. Tho. 2.
2. q. 82.
art. 3.

ANOTHER great benefit & profit there is, as *S. Thomas* sayth, in *Meditation*; and it is, that true *Deuotion* springs from thence; a thing so important in spirituall life, and so much desired by all them who walke that way. *Deuotion* is no other thing, but a *Promptitude and readinesse of will, towards all that, which is good.* And therefore a deuoute man is he, who is ready and disposed for all goodnesse. And this is the generall doctrine of the *Saints. S. Thomas* sayth moreouer, that there are two causes of this *Deuotion*, the one is *extrinsecall* which is God, & that is the principall. The other is *intrinsecall* on our part, which is *Meditation.* For this *prompt and ready will*, towards the actiōs of vertue, doth grow from the *consideration,* and *Meditation* of the *Vnderstanding,*

ding; and this is that, which next after the grace of God, may be truly said to kindle and blow the fire in our hart.

So that true *Deuotion* and feruour of **Note?** spirit, doth not confiste in the sweetnes and sensible guste, wherof some haue experience, and sense in *Prayer;* but in hauing a *will,* which is *prompte* and *ready preſt,* towards all those things which concerne the seruice of Almighty God. And this is the *deuotion,* which continues and lasts, whilest the other comes quickly to an end. For that, doth but consist of certaine affects of sensible deuotion, which rise from a quicke desire, which one hath, of any thing which is desirable, and amiable. And many tymes it proceedeth from a mans naturall complexiō, in that he hath a sweet disposition, and a tender hart, which is quickly moued towards softnesse, and tears; & when this kind of deuotion is once dropped downe, the good purposes, are assoone dryed vp. This is but a téder kind of loue, which is grounded in gustes, and consolations; and as long as that guste, and deuotion lasts, the

E 3 man

man wilbe very diligent, and punctuall; and he wilbe a friend of silence, and recolection. But when that deuotion is ended, there is an end of all. Whereas they, who are so grounded in *Truth*, by meanes of *Meditation* and *consideration*; and are conuinced, & disabused by solide reason; these are the men, who continue and perseuere in vertue: and although those gustes & consolations faile them, yet they are still the same, that they were before: because the same cause and reason lasts, which at the first induced, & moued them to it.

This is a masculine, & strong kind of loue, and by this *Touch of triall*, the true seruants of God are seene: & not in those gusts, and consolations. They are wonte to say, that our passions are like certaine little dogs, which stand barking at vs; and in the tyme of spirituall consolation, they haue their mouthes muzled vp. And make account that God doth caste certaine bits of bread, before euery one of them, and with that, they are quiet, & craue nothing: but take you away that bread

of

of confolation, and then one of them,
will begin to barke, and the other of
them wilbe as fure to follow, and then
is the tyme to fee, how euery one doth
carry himfelfe . They alfo compare
thefe guftes, and confolations, to *mo-
ueable goods*, & *chattels*, which are foone
fpent: but folide vertues, are as *freehold* ,
or *land of inheritance*, which continues
and lafts, & fo they are of more price.

From hence groweth a *Truth*, wherof we take experience many tymes, &
it is worthy of confideration. We fee **Note**
fome perfons , who on the one fide,
haue great comforts in their *Prayer*; and
afterward, in temptations & other occafions of finne, we fee them weake,
and fallen. And on the contrary part,
we fee others, who fuffer great dry-
neffe in *Prayer* , and know not what
belongs to any fpirituall confolation,
or gufte; and yet we find thefe laft, to
be ftronge, when they are tempted, &
far from falling. The caufe of this , is
that, which we were faying before.
That the former fort of men , did
ground themfelues in gufts , and in-
waŕde feelings; but the latter, laide

E 4 their

their foundation vpon reason, & were
disabused, conuinced, and possessed
with the reall truth of things; and with
that, they last, and perseuere in those
things, which formerly they did resolue.

So that one of the meanes, and that
a very good one, which viually we
giue, to make men perseuere, in those
good purposes which they conceiue in
Note.   *Prayer*, and to put them in execution,
is; That men must procure to conserue
in memory, the motiue and reason,
which caused that good desire, and
purpose in them, formerly; for that
which moued them before, to desire it,
will helpe them afterwards to conserue, & put it in execution. Nay there
is more in this, then what is said. For
when a man goeth thus *vnbeguiling*, &
conuincing himselfe, in *Prayer*, although
afterward he remember not particulerly the *medium*, or *reason* which moued him then, yet in vertue of his hauing beene *vnbeguiled* before, and of
the resolution which then he tooke,
being conuinced by truth and reason
he continueth firme and strong, to
re sist

refift the temptation afterward, and to perfeuere in vertue.

Therefore doth Gerfon, efteeme fo much of *Meditation.* For being confulted about, what exercife might be more vfefull, or profitable to a *Religious man,* who liueth recolected in his *Cell,* eyther *reading,* or *vocall Prayer,* or fome worke of the hand, or els to attend to *Meditation;* he anfwered, that (fauing the duty which they owe to *Obedience*)they were beft attend to *Meditation.* And he giues this reafon therof; That although by meanes of *Vocall Prayer,* or reading of fome fpirituall booke, a man, for the prefent, may peraduenture find greater profit, and deuotion, then by meanes of *Meditation;* yet in giuing ouer to *pray vocally,* or laying the booke afide, that deuotion may quickly be at an end; whereas *Meditation* doth profit, and difpofe men well, for the future. And therfore he fayth, That it is fit, that we accuftome our felues to *Meditation;* to the end, that although the found of wordes, and the fight of bookes may faile vs; yet *Meditation* may be our booke, and

Gerfon p. 1. alphab. 34 litera M. & de follicitudine religiofa. p. 41. alpha. 6. 37.lit. A

and ſo we may not want true deuotion.

CHAP. XI.

Of the manner, which we are to hold in
Prayer, *and of the* Fruite *we are to*
gather thence.

Pſal. 38. 4. CONCALVIT *cor meum intra me,*
& in meditatione mea exardeſcit ignis.
In theſe words, the Prophet *Dauid* teacheth vs, the manner which we are to
hold in *Prayer*, according to the expli-
Hieron.   cation of many *Doctors*, and *Saints*, who
Ambroſ.   interpret this place, of the *fire of Chari-*
Greg. li. *ty*, and the loue of God, & our neigh-
23 mor. c. bour; which was kindled by the *Medi-*
5. interlin. *tation* of heauenly things, & did burne
& alij.   in the breſt, of the *Royall Prophet.* My
hart ſayth he, grew into heat, & was
all kindled within me. This is the effect of *Prayer.* But how got he this
heat? How did that fire come to kindle
it ſelfe, in his hart? Will you know
how? It was by meanes of *Meditation.*
Et in meditatione mea exardeſcit ignis. This
is the meanes, and the inſtrument, for
the

the kindling of this fire. So that as *S. Cyrill of Alexandria* fayth, *Meditation is as the steele which giues against the flint, to the end that fire may be produced.* By difcourfe and *Meditation* of the *Vnderstanding*, you are to ftrike vpon the hard *steele* of your *hart*; till fuch tyme as the *loue of God* may be kindled in it; & a defire be produced of humility, of mortification, and the reft of the vertues; & you are not to giue ouer, till you haue kindled, and bred this *fire*.

Cyrillus Alexandrinus.

Although *Meditation* be very good, and neceffary, yet the whole tyme of *Prayer*, is not to paffe away in difcourfe, and confideration of the *Vnderstanding*; neither are we to dwell in that; for this would be rather *study*, then *Prayer*. But all the *Meditations* and *confiderations* which we are to haue, muft be taken, but as a meanes for the awaking, and kindling thefe affects, and defires of vertue, in our hart. For the fanctity and perfection of a Chriftian life, doth not confift only in good thoughts, nor in the intelligence of holy things, but in found, and folide vertue; and efpecially in the acts, and opera-

S. Tho. 1.
2. q. 3. art.
9.
operations therof; wherin, as *S. Thomas* sayth, *the last perfection of vertue doth consist;* and so we must principally imploy our selues, and insist vpon the procuring of this, in our tyme of *Prayer.*

Note.

This is therfore to be our first principle in this matter. Yea, and euen the *Philosopher* sayth (which is alledged by Gerson super Mag-
nificat. al-
phab. 86.
litera D. Gerson) *Inquirimus quid sit virtus, non vt sciamus, sed vt boni efficiamur.* We go inquiring, and searching after the knowing what vertue is; not to the end that we may be more learned, but that we may become good, and vertuous. Thogh the needle be necessary to sow withall; yet it is not the needle, which sticheth two things togeather, but the thred. And so should he be very indiscreet, who would passe the needle in and out, without thred, for this should be, to labour in vayne. And yet this very thing they do, who in *Prayer,* attend only to *meditating,* and *vnderstanding,* and little to *louing. Meditation* is to be as the *needle,* which is to enter first; but it must be, to the end, that the *thred of loue,* and the affection of our will, may follow after; wherby he must
ioyne,

ioyne, & vnite our selues, to Almighty God.

Our *B. F. Ignatius*, doth put vs in
mind herof, after a very particuler māner. After he had placed the *Poynts*,
which we are to meditate, with some
very short considerations vpon them,
he then sayth, these words: And I am to
apply all this to my selfe, to th'end that
I may reape some fruite therby. In this
the *Fruite* of Prayer doth consist, that
men may know how to referre, & apply that which they *meditate* to themselues; euery one, according as he hath
need. The glorious *S. Bernard* sayth
very well, that as the *Sunne* doth not
heat euery one whome it illuminates;
so *Knowledge*, and *Meditation* (althouh
it teach that; which is to be done) yet
doth it not moue all men, nor breed an
affection in them, to do that which
they are taught. One thing it is, to
haue notice of great riches, and another to possesse them. That which makes men rich, is not the hauing notice
of riches, but the possessing them. So
is it (sayth he) one thing to know God
and another thing to feare and loue
him;

Bern. serm. 23. super Cantica.

him ; and the *knowing* many things of God, doth not make vs true *Saints*, and spiritually rich ; but the *louing* and fearing of God. He bringeth also another good cōparison to this purpose ; That as he who is hungry, shall help himselfe but a little, by placing before himselfe, a large table full of exquisite and choyce meates, if he eate none of them; so he who vseth Prayer, shalbe litle the better for hauing a sumptuous, and curious table, set before him, full of excellent, and choyce considerations ; if he do not feed thereupon, by applying them to himselfe, with his *Will*.

That we may descend a litle more to particulers , I say , That the thing which we are to draw out of *Meditation*, and *Prayer*, is to be , Holy affections and desires, which are framed first interiorly in the hart, and afterwards are put in practise , in due tyme. The Bleßed *S. Ambrose* sayth, That *action is the end of Meditation. Meditationis præceptorum cælestium intentio, vel finis operatio est*. Those holy & *Mysterious beasts* (which the Prophet *Ezechiel* saw) amongst other conditions of theirs, had *wings* , as
he

Nota.

*Ambros.
in Pf. 118.
super illud
Et meditabar in præceptis tuis.
Ezech.1.8.*

he fayth, and vnder them, they had the
bands of a man. *Et manus hominis, fub*
pennis eorum ; to giue vs to vnderstand,
that the flying, and difcourfing with
the *Vnderftanding*, muft be directed to
working. We muft therfore fetch from
Prayer, affects and defires of humility ;
defpifing our felues, and defiring to be
defpifed by others. Defires of fuffering
paine, and troubles, for the loue of
God; and being glad of fuch, as at the
prefent, lye vpon vs. Defires of pouerty
of fpirit, wifhing that the worft things
of the houfe may be for vs ; and that
fomething may be wanting to vs,
euen of thofe which are neceffary.
Griefe, and contrition for finnes; and
firme purpofes, rather to burft, then to
finne againe. Gratitude for benefits
receiued, and true intiere refignatiō into the hands of God. And finally, a
defire to imitate Chrift our Lord, and
our Maifter, in all thofe vertues, which
fhine fo brightly in his life. To this
muft our *Meditation* be addreffed and
ordeyned; and this is the fruite, which
we muft draw from thence.

Vpon this it followes, That fince Note,
we

we take *Meditation*, and the difcourfe of
our *Vnderſtanding* for a *meanes* to moue
our *Will* to thefe affections; & that this
is the *end* of this bufineffe; we muſt fo
far vfe *Meditation*, and the difcourfe of
our *Vnderſtanding*, as fhall be fit for this
end, and no further. For the *meanes* are
to carry a proportion, and to receaue
their meafure from the *end*; and fo
when we finde our *Will* moued, and
mollified with fome good affection to
any vertue, as namely to *griefe for finnes, contempt of the world, loue of God, defire
to fuffer for his fake*, or the like, we muſt
prefently cut off the thred of the difcourfe of the *Vnderſtanding*, as a man
would draw a Bridge, from before a
paffenger; and we muſt detayne our
felues, and paufe vpon that affection,
and defire of our *Will*, till fuch tyme as
we be fatisfyed, & till we haue drunke
it deeply downe, into our foules.

P. N. Ig-
natius lib.
Exercitio-
rum fpiri-
tual. addit.
4.

    This is a very important aduife; &
our *B. Father*, doth place it in his booke
of *fpirituall Exercifes*, where he fayth;
That as foone as we haue found that
deuotion, and feeling which we defire, we are then to paufe, and to deteyne

teyne our felues therein , without hauing anxiety of paffing towards any
thinge els, till we remaine fully fatif-
fyed. Iuft fo, as the *Gardner*, when he   Note.
will water a *peece* of ground, as foone
as the *water* is entred in vpon it, he de-
teynes the thred of the current , and
giues it meanes to foake , & imbrue it
felfe in the intralls of that dry foyle; &
till that be fufficiently done, he fuffers
not the water to paffe away. So when
the water of good affections and defires, beginnes to enter into the foule,
which is as *earth without water*, according to that of the Prophet, *Anima mea*   Pfa.142.6.
ficut terra fine aqua tibi: we are to deteyne
the current of the difcourfe, and *Vnder-*
standing, and to remayne, enioying that
motion and affection of our will, as
long as we can; till fuch tyme, as our
hart may be bathed, and imbrued ther-
with, and fo we may remaine fully fatisfyed. The B. *Saint Iohn Chryfoftome*,   Chryfof.
brings another good comparifon, to   tome.
declare this. Haft thou feene (fayth   »
he) when the little lambe, goes to   »
feeke the breft of his dame? what doth   »
it but ftir, and feeke, heere and there, &

F   now

now takes the tet, and then leaues it.
But when once the ftreame of milke
comes clere, the lambe is prefently at
a pawfe, and doth enioy the milke at
eafe. So is it in the cafe of Prayer. For
till that dew come from heauen, the
man goes difcourfing heere and there.
But whē once that heauenly dew def-
cends, we are prefently to pawfe, and
to enioy that delight, and fweetneffe.

Chap. XII.

Of how great importance it is, to deteyne our
felues, in the acts, & affections
of our Will.

IT is of great importance, do te-
teyne our felues, and to make a
ftand, in the acts and affections of the
Will. And the *Saints,* and Maifters of
fpirituall life, do efteeme of it fo much,
as to fay, that in this confifteth, good
and perfect Prayer; yea and that alfo,
which they call *Contemplation;* when a
man no longer is feeking incentiues
of *Prayer,* by *Meditation,* but ftands in-
ioying that loue, which he hath foght
                                    and

and found; and doth repose therein, as in the *end* of his inquisition, and desire: saying with the *Spouse* in the Canticles, *Inueni, queam diligit anima mea; tenui eum, nec dimittam.* I haue found him whome my soule loues; I haue him, and I will hold him fast. And this is also that, which the *Spouse* sayth in the same place, *Ego dormio, & cor meum vigilat;* I sleepe, but my hart is well awake. For in perfect *Prayer*, the *Vnderstanding* is laide, as it were to sleepe, because discourse, and speculation being lefte, the *Will* is both watching, and euen melting, with the loue of her fellow *Spouse*. And he, likes this sleepe of hers so well, that he commaunds it to be nourished in her, *and that she may not be awaked, till she will her selfe. Adiuro vos filia Ierusalem per capreas, ceruosq; camporum, ne suscitetis, neque euigilare faciatis dilectam, donec ipsa velit.* In such sort, that *Meditation*, and all those other parts, which they touch of *Prayer*, be ordeyned, and addressed to this *Contemplation*; and are, as it were, the ladders, wherby we clyme vp to it. So sayth *S. Augustine*, in a booke, which he calleth the

Cant. 3. 4.

Cant. 5. 2

Cant. 3. 5.

August. de scala Paradisi.

the *ladder of Paradise* : *Lectio inquirit, meditatio inuenit, oratio postulat , contemplatio degustat.* Reading seeks, Meditation findes , Prayer desires, but Contemplation enioyes, and gustes , that which was sought, desired, and found. And he brings that of the Gospell , *Quærite & iuuenietis, pulsate & aperietur vobis.* Seeke by reading, and you shall find by meditating; knock by Prayer, & it shalbe opened vnto you, by Contemplation. And the *Saints* obserue, and *Albertus Magnus* doth alledge it, that this is the difference betweene the *Contemplation* of *Faythfull Catholiks,* and that of *heathen Philosophers*; That the *Contemplation* of the *Philosophers* was wholy addressed towards the perfecting of the *Vnderstanding,* by the knowledge of such *truthes* as might be knowne; and so it did end in the *Vnderstanding* ; for this is the end therof, to *know,* and know more, & yet more, then that . But the *Contemplation* of *Catholikes* and of *Saints* (wherof now we treat) doth not rest in the *Vnderstanding,* but passeth on to moue, and rectify, and enkindle, & inflame the *Will,* with the loue of God, according

ding

Matt.7.7.

Albertus magnus l. de adherendo Deo ca. 9.
Note.

ding to that of the *Spouse: Anima mea li-*   *Cant. 5. 6.*
quefacta est , vt loquutus est. My soule did
euen melt, as soone as my beloued be-
gan to speake. And *S. Thomas* treating   *S. Tho. 2*
of *Contemplation,* noteth this very well,   *2. q. 180.*
and sayth : That howsoeuer *Contem-*   *art. 7.*
plation doth essentially consist in the
Vnderstanding ; yet that the last Perfection therof, is *in Loue,* and in the affection of the *Will,* so that the chiefe in-
tent, and end of our *Contemplation,* is to
be the affect of the *Will,* and the *loue of*
God.

In this sort (sayth *S. Augustine*) did   *Aug. lib.*
Christ our Lord teach vs to pray,   *de orando*
when he said in his Gospell, *Orantes*   *Deum ca.*
autem, nolite multùm loqui; when ye pray   *10. quæ est*
talke not much. *S. Augustine* sayth also: *Epistola*
Aliud est sermo multus, aliud diuturnus af-   *121. ad*
fectus; absit ab oratione multa loquutio, sed   *Probum.*
non desit multa precatio. One thing it is to   *Matt. 6.*
speake much, and to discourse, and
flourish much with the Vnderstanding ; and another thing it is to de-   "
teyne our selues much in affects of the   "
Will, and in the acts of Loue. That   "
which he mentioneth first, which is   "
to talke much, we are to procure to de-   "
    F 3   cline,

cline, and auoid in *Prayer*. *Et negotium hoc, plus gemitibus quàm sermonibus agitur;* and this businesse of Prayer (sayth the Saint,) is not a businesse of much talke, nor shall we in Prayer, negotiate so well with Almighty God, by figures, nor plenty of discourse, not delicacy of conceits, as with tears, and sighs, and groanes, and profound desires of the hart, according to that of the prophet *Ieremias: Neque taceat pupilla oculi tui.* Let not the apple of thine eye be silent. *S. Hierome*, vpon these words, askes the question, how the Prophet could say, *That the apple of the eye must not be silent. Is not the tongue* (sayth he) *that which speakes? how then can speach be vsed, by the apple of the eye?* The Saint answers thus. *When we shed tears in the sight of God, it is then rightly said, that the apple of our eye cryes out to him: for howsoeuer we speake not a word with our tongue, without hart we may cry out to God.* So sayth *S. Paul, Misit Deus spiritum filij sui in corda vestra, clamantem, Abba pater.* And in *Exodus* God said to *Moyses, Quid clamas ad me? Why dost thou cry out to me?* & yet he spake not a word, but only, in his

Tren. 2. *18.*
Hieron. in *Psa. 50.*

Ad Gal. *4. 6.*

Exodus *14. 15.*

his hart he prayed, with so great feruour & efficacy, that God said to him,
why dost thou so cry out, before me? Let vs
also thus cry out to God, in Prayer,
with our eyes (*Neque iaceat pupilla oculi
tui*) with tears, with sighes, with groanes, and with the deepe desire of our
harts.

Chap. XIII.

*Wherein satisfaction is giuen to their com-
plaints, who say, that they cannot, nor
know not how to Meditate, nor discourse
with their Vnderstanding.*

HERBY we shall easily answere,
to a very common complaint
of some, who afflict themselues with
saying, That they know not how to
discourse in Prayer, becaufe they meete
with no confiderations which they
can dilate; and that they know not
how to extend the *Points*, but that instantly the threed is cut off.

There is no cause, why any body
should be in paine for this. For (as I
haue said already) this businesse of

Prayer,

Prayer, confifteth more in the affects, and defires of the *Will*, then in the difcourfe, and fpeculation of the *Vnderftanding*. Nay the teachers of fpirituall life, do aduife here, that we muft take care, that the *Meditation* of the *Vnderftanding*, be not too much ; becaufe this vfeth to giue great hinderance to the motion, & affection of the *Will*, which ought to be the chiefe. And efpecially, when one deteyneth himfelfe in certaine confiderations, which are curious and fubtile, the *Will* is hindred fo much the more. The reafon herof is naturall. For it is cleere, that in a fountaine, which makes but one channell of water, and hath many pipes, which conduct and carry it feuerall wayes; how much more water runs by one of them, fo much the leffe , will run by the other. Now the power of the *Soule* is bounded, and limitted ; and how much more water runs by the pipe of the *Vnderftanding*, fo much leffe will run, by that of the *Will*.

And fo we fee by experience, that if the foule be in deuotion , and tendernesse, & that the *Vnderftanding* will
                                            offer

Note.

offer then to range abroad , by any
curiofity & fpeculation , the hart doth
inſtantly grow dry, and the deuotion
decayes, becauſe all the water is runne
into the pipe of the *Vnderſtanding* , and
therfore that of the *Will* remaineth dry.
And ſo ſayth *Gerſon*, that it growes fro
hence, that they who are not ſo learned, are ſometymes , yea and very often , more deuoute , and more happy
in *Prayer* , then they who are learned;
becauſe they leake leſſe, towards their
Vnderſtanding part; not imploying nor
diſtracting themſelues in ſpeculations,
or curioſityes; but inſtantly procuring
with playne and clere conſiderations ,
to affect and moue the *Will* And thoſe
humble, and homely reflections do
moue them more , and worke greater
effects vpon their mindes, then more
high and curious conceytes do , vpon
the mind of others . As we ſee in the
the perſon of that holy *Cooke* , (of
whome I ſpake els where) who from
the materiall fire which he vſed ſo
much , tooke occaſion to be ſtill thinking of the eternall fire of hell ; & this
he did with ſo great deuotion , that he
had

Gerſon p. 3. de monte contempl. alph. 73. c. 2. & ſequent.

Tract. 3. 8.

had the guift of teares, in the middeft of all his bufineffe.

And this which followes muft be much noted. For, fo the affect, and defire, be very high and fpirituall, it matters not a whit, though the conceyt and confideration, be meane and common. We haue expetience inough of this, in holy *Scripture*; where the Holy Ghoft declareth to vs very high, and fublime things, by common, & playne confiderations, vpon thefe words, *Quis dabit mihi pennas ficut columba, & volabo, & requiefcam* ? Who will giue me the wings of a Doue, that I may fly vp and reft? *S. Ambrofe* afketh why the Prophet, defiring to fly vp, and reach to the higheft, fhould defire the *wings of a Doue*, rather then of fome other bird, fince there are other birds who are fpeedier of the wing, then the Doue ? And he anfwereth, that the Prophet did it, becaufe he deemed the wings of a *Doue* were beft for one that meant to fly high, towards perfection, and to obtayne the guift of perfect, & high Prayer; that is to fay, that harmeleffe, & plaine people of hart, were

fitter

Pfal.54.7.

Ambr.fer. 70.

Note.

fitter for it , then these sharpe and curious Vnderstandings , according to that of the Wise-man, *Et cum simplicibus sermocinatio eius.* They are humble & plaine people of hart, to whome God loues to communicate himselfe. Pro. 3: 32.

So that no man is to be troubled, in regard that he is not able to discourse, nor finde Considerations, nor dilate the points of his *Meditation.* Nay rather they say, and with much reason, that it is better for them , and that their lot is fallen into fairer and richer ground, to whome Almighty God doth stop the veyne of superfluous speculations, and doth open that of the affection; to the end, that with a peaceable and quiet vnderstanding, the will may repose & rest in God alone , imploying all her loue, and ioy , vpon that soueraigne Good. If our Lord do you so great fauour, as by the meanes of one playne and simple consideration, or with only thinking how God made himselfe man , and that he was borne in a stable; and laid in no better then a manger, and that he lodged himselfe vpon a *Crosse,* for you ; to inflame you in the loue Note loue of his diuine maieſty, and in a deſire to humble, and mortify your ſelues for his ſake; and if you can imploy the whole hower, and many howers in this; much better, and more profitable *Prayer* it is, then if you had made many diſcourſes, and conſiderations, which were very curious, & ſublyme. For thus you imploy, & deteyne your ſelues in the beſt, and moſt ſubſtantiall part of *Prayer*, and that which is indeed the end and fruite therof. Wherby the errour of ſome is eaſily vnderſtood, who when they find not out certaine conſiderations, wherin they can deteyne themſelues long, do not thinke that they make good *Prayer*, & when they meete with ſtore of matter of that kind, they thinke it is excellent.

In the Cronicles of *S. Francis*, it is recounted, how the holy man *Brother Giles*, ſaid thus to *S. Bonauenture*, who then was the *Generall* of his Order: *Great mercy did God ſhew to you, learned men, and great meanes did he giue you, wherwith to ſerue and praiſe his diuine Maieſty; but we ignorant and ſimple people, who haue no parts of wit or learning; what can we do,*
                       which

which may be pleasing to Almighty God? S. *Bonauenture* answered; *If our Lord did no other fauour to man, then that he might be inabled to loue him; this alone were sufficient to oblige him to do God greater seruice, then all the rest put togeather.* The holy Brother *Giles* replyed thus : *And can then, an ignorant person loue our Lord Iesus Christ , aswell a learned man ? Yea* (sayth S. Bonauenture,) *a poore old simple woman , may perhaps loue our Lord better, then a great Doctor of Diuinity.* The holy brother *Giles* rose instantly vp, with great feruour, and went into that part of the Garden, which looked towards the Towne; and with a strong voyce cryed out, *O thou poore, thou ignorant, and simple old woman, loue thy Lord Iesus Christ, and perhaps thou shalt grow greater in heauen, then Brother Bonauenture.* And he remained rapt in *Extasis,* as he vsed to be, without stirring from that place , in three howers .

CHAP.

Chap. XIV.

Of two directions which wilbe of much help to vs, for the procuringe to make good Prayer, *and to reape much Fruite therby.*

Note

TO the end, that we may make our *Prayer* well, and gather that *Fruite* therby, which is fit; it will helpe vs much, if we vnderstand, and go alwaies vpon this *Ground.* That *Prayer* is not the end, but the meanes which we are to take for our profit, & perfection: So that we must not enter vpon *Prayer,* as meaning to make that our last designe. For the perfection of our soules, doth not cōsist in hauing great consolation, and sweetnes, and *Contemplation;* but in obteyning a perfect mortification, and victory ouer our seiues, and ouer our passions, and appetites ; reducing our soules (asmuch as possibly we can)to that happy state of *Originall Iustice,* wherin they were created, when our *sense* and appetite was wholy subiect and conforme to *reason,* and *reason* to *God.* Now we are to

take

take *Prayer*, for the *meanes* of attaining to this *end*.

Iron is made softe , betweene the *Anuile* and the *fire*, to the end that they may worke it, and double it, and do with it what they list ; and iust so it is to be in *Prayer*. To the end that we may not find mortification very difficult and offensiue, but that we may be ableto breake our selues of our owne will, and to be content with trouble, as occasion is offered ; we had need come to the anuile of *Prayer*, and there with the heat and fire of deuotion, and by the example of Christ our Lord, out hart goes softning it selfe , that so we may worke, and mould it towards any thing that shalbe fit for the greater seruice, and glory of God .

This is the duty of *Prayer*, and this is the Fruit, which we must reape frō thence. And for this purpose it is, that our Lord is wont to giue consolation, and gust in *Prayer*; not to the end that we may stay there; but that we may fly on, by the way of vertue , towards perfection, with the greater alacrity, and speed.

This

This is that which the holy ghost
meant to giue vs to vnderstand, in that
which happened to *Moyses*, when he
came downe from speaking with Almighty God. The holy Scripture sayth,
That he came forth with great splendor in his face; and it noteth, that the
same *splendor* appeared, after the māner
of *hornes*, in which the strégth of beasts
doth consist: to giue vs to vnderstand,
that we are to draw strength frō *Praier*,
wherby we may worke well . The
same Truth, did Christ our Lord teach
vs, by his example, in the night of his
Passion , resorting to the help of *Prayer*,
once, twice, & thrice; to prouide himselfe so, for his combat, which then he
foūd to be at hād. Not that himselfe had
any need therof, as *S. Ambrose* notes; but
to giue example to vs. And the holy
Gospell sayth , *that an Angell appeared* ,
who gaue him comfort; and he rose from
Prayer , so full of strength, that insiāt-
ly he sayd to his disciples , *Surgite, ea-*
mus , *ecce appropinquauit, qui me tradet* .
Rise vp, let vs go, and meete our enemyes, for behold he approacheth, who
will betray me . He maketh offer of
                                        himselfe

Psa. 118.
32.

Exodus
34.29.

Ambro-
sius.
Lucæ. 6.
Luc. 22.
43.

Matt. 26.
46.
Isa. 53. 7.

himselfe, and deliuereth himselfe vp
into their hands: *Oblatus est quia ipse vo-*
luit. All this serues, but to teach vs, that
we must take *Prayer*, as the meanes to
ouercome those difficultyes, which
present themselues, in the way of
vertue.

S. *Iohn Chrysostome* sayth, that *Prayer* Chryso-
is a kind of tempering, and tuning the steme.
Violl of our hart, that so it may make Note.
good musicke, in the eares of Almighty
God. Our businesse therfore in *Prayer*,
must be, to moderate, and tune the
cords of our passions, and affections,
and of all our actions; to the end that
they all, may stand well with reason,
and with God. And this is that which
we are saying daily; & which we also
here others say, in their sermons, and
spirituall exhortations, that our *Prayer*
must be *Practicall*: That is, it must be
addressed to working, and must helpe
vs to make those difficultyes smooth,
and those repugnances weake, which
obiect themselues to vs, in a spirituall
life. And for this reason, the holy
Ghost called it *Prudence*: *Scientia Sancto-* Pro. 9. 1o.
rum Prudentia. For *Prudence* is addres-
G   sed

sed to *working* ; to shew the difference
of this, from the *science* of learned men,
which only consisteth in *knowing*. And
so the *Saints* affirme, that *Prayer* is the
generall, and most efficacious remedy,
against all our temptations, and all
other necessityes, and to all the occasions, which may be offered. And this
is one of the chiefe commendations,
which belong to *Prayer*.

Theodo-
ret.
Note.
    Theodoret relates in his religious Hi-
story, of a holy *Monke*, who said, that
Phisitians cure seuerall diseases of the
body, euery one with a seuerall remedy, nay, that many tymes for the cure
of one disease, they apply many remedyes; for in fine remedyes fall short, &
their vertue is lymitted, and abrid-
ged. But *Prayer*, is a remedy both vni-
uersall, and full of efficacy; against all
necessityes, and to resist all temptations, and bad encounters of the enemy, and to obteyne all vertue; and to
apply vnto the soule, an infinite good,
which is God. For vpon him it takes
hold, and in him it rests, and so they
call *Prayer*, *Omnipotent*. *Omnipotens oratio, cùm sit vna, omnia potest*. And Christ
                      our

our Redeemer, againſt all temptatiõs,
gaue vs this remedy of Prayer. *Vigilate*
& orate , vt non intretis in tentationem.
Watch,& pray, leſt you enter into temptatõ.

The ſecond aduiſe,which will alſo
ſerue vs much, for the execution of
that which hath beene ſaid, is, That as
when we go to *Prayer*, we muſt be
prouided of the *Points*, wherupon we
meane to *meditate*; ſo alſo we muſt for-
thinke the *Fruite*, which we deſire to
drawfrom thence. But ſome will ſay,
how ſhall we know what *Fruite* we
are to draw, out of Prayer, before we
beginne to make it? We deſire that
you would declare this to vs, more at
large. Content. Did we not ſay euen
now, that we muſt go to Prayer in
ſearch after a remedy of our ſpirituall
neceſſityes, and to obtayne the victory of our ſelues,& ouer our paſſions, &
euill inclinations ; and that Prayer, is
the meanes which we are to take for
our reformation and amendement?
Well then ; before any man enter into
Prayer he is to conſider thus with himſelfe, at good leaſure. What is the greateſt ſpirituall neceſſity, that I am ſub-

Matth.26.
41.

Chap. 22.

Note.

G 2   iect

iect too : What is that, which hindreth my proceeding most, and maketh most warre agaynst my soule. And this is that, which we are to thinke of before; and to place it before our eyes, & to insist vpon it ; to fetch the remedy thereof, out of our Prayer. And the prouiding and preparing of the *Points* of our *Meditation* must be addressed to that purpose. I wil giue you an exaple.

I finde in my selfe, a great inclination to be valued and esteemed, and that men should make much accompt of me ; and that humaine respects vse to transport me much ; and that, when any occasion is offered, whereby my selfe to be vndervalued, I feele it, and I am troubled much, and perhaps somtymes, I make show therof. This me thinkes is that, which makes stiffest war against me, and that which most hindreth my proceeding in spirit, and the peace and quietnes of my soule, and makes me fall into the greatest faults.

Well, if your greatest necessity consist in this, *remedy* must stand in ouercoming, and rooting vp this imperfection.

ction. And this is that which you are to carry in your mind, & that which you are to place before your eyes; & to take it to hart, and to infist vpon it, that fo you may obteyne it by Prayer. And fo it is an errour, for one to go ordinarily to God, in Prayer, as by chance; to take hold of that, which fhall there prefent it felfe, (like a Woodman who would fhoote at the *Heard*, let the arrow light where it wil) leauing that a part, wherof he ftandeth in greateft need. But the truth is, that we muft not go to Prayer, to take that which comes, but to procure that, which is for our purpofe.

The fick man, when he goes into the Apothecaryes fhop, layes not hold **Note** vpon the firft drugge he findes; but vpon that wherof he hath need, for his infirmity. There is one man, who is full of pride vp to the very eyes, another of impatience, another of ftiffe Iudgment, and felfe conceit, as is daily feene when any occafion is offered, & he takes himfelfe dayly in the manner; and yet he goes vpon Prayer, to flourifh, and make fyne conceyts; and he

he layes hold vpon that which firſt
comes in his way, or which giues him
moſt guſt ; picking heere, and there.

This is not the way to gather *Fruite.*
A man is alwayes to obſerue well,
what it is which he needeth moſt, and
to procure the remedy, ſince he goes to
Prayer for that end. *S. Ephrem* brings
to this purpoſe, the Example of that
blinde man in the Goſpell , who came
calling, and crying out , to Chriſte
our Lord, *that he would haue mercy on him.*
Conſider (ſayth he) how Chriſt demanding of him , what it was that he
deſired ? the blind man did inſtantly
repreſent his greateſt neceſſity, & that
which gaue him moſt payne , which
was his want of ſight; and of that , he
deſired to be deliuered : *Dominus vt vi-
deam.* Doth he perhaps demand any o-
ther of thoſe things, wherof yet indeed
he might haue need ? Did he ſay perhaps, *Lord giue me ſome cloathes, for I am
poore?* He askes not that ; but , laying
aſide all other things, he reſorts to the
thought of his greateſt neceſſity. So are
we (ſayth he) to do in Prayer, conſi-
dering wherof we haue moſt need, in-
ſiſting

*Ephrem.
exhort. ad
Religioſus
de armatu-
ra ſpiri-
tuali l. 2.
pag. 160.*

Luc. 18.

*Marc. 10.
51.*

Of Mentall Prayer.

103

therof, till we obteyne it.

To the end that there may be no
excuse in this, it is to be noted. That
howsoeuer it be true, that when he
who goes to Prayer, and pretends to
produce desires of the particuler vertues which wanteth most, is ordinarily to procure, that the *Points*, & matter vpon which he will meditate, may
carry some conueniency, and proportion therunto; to the end that the *Will*
may be the more quickly moued (and
that with greater constancy and feruour)to the producing of those desires;
and so, may the more easily obteyne
the Fruite, which he expects; yet it
is also fit to be vnderstood, that whatsoeuer Exercise a man makes, & whatsoeuer *Mistery* he meditates, he may yet
apply it, to that which he needeth
most. For Prayer is as the *Mana* of heauen, which sauours to euery one, as
himselfe will. If yow would haue it
sauour of *Humility*, or of the *Consideration of sinne*,or *death*, or of the *passion of
our Lord*, or of *benefits receyued*; if you
will draw from hence much *griefe*, or

G 4

Confu-

Confuſion for your Offencès, it will fauour of any of theſe things. It will alſo
ſauour of *Patience* , if that be the thing,
which you would ſtriue to get; &ſo in
the reſt.

Chap. XV.

*How it is to be vnderſtood, that in Prayer we
are to take ſome one thing to hart , wherof we haue greateſt neede, wherein we
muſt inſiſt till we obtaine it .*

I Will not ſay for all this , that we
muſt euer attend to one, & the ſame
thing in Prayer . Becauſe howſoeuer
our greateſt particuler neceſſity may
be the want of *humility,* or the like, yet
we may well imploy our ſelues in
Prayer , vpon the acts and exerciſes
alſo of other vertues. An occaſion pre-
ſents it ſelfe to you of coforming your
ſelues to the will of God, in all that
which he ſhall diſpoſe, and ordayne
cocerning you; deteyne your ſelues in
it , as long as you can ; for this will
be a very good Prayer, and very well
imployed , and will no way blunt the
lance , wherewith you meane to take
Humility , but will rather ſharpen the
point therof.   It

It comes to your minde, to make a greate act of acknowledgment, and gratitude, for the benefits which you Note. haue receyued from God, afwell in generall, as particuler; deteyne your felues alfo herein, for it is great reafon, that we fhould dayly thanke our Lord for the benefits which we haue receyued; & efpecially, for hauing drawne vs to the ftate of Religion. It occurs to you to make an act of deteftation of your fins, & of much griefe for hauing comitted them;& of *firme purpofe* rather to dy a thoufand tymes then to offend God any more: deteyne your felues herein; for it is one of the beft, & moft profitable acts, which you are able to exercife in your Prayer. It comes into your minde, to make an act of great *loue of God, and of zeale,* and great defire of the faluation of foules, and to endure any trouble for them; deteyne your felues alfo herein; and heere you may alfo well deteyne your felues in defiring fauour of Almighty God, not onely for your owne foules, but for your neighbours, and for the whole *Church*; For this is one, and that a very

piinprincipall part of Prayer. In all thefe things, and in the like to thefe, we may well deteyne our felues, and it wilbe a very profitable Prayer. And fo we fee, that the Pfalms, which are a moft perfect kind of Prayer, are full of very different affects. For this reafon, *Caffian*, & the *Abbot Nilus* fayd, that Prayer was like a *field full of plants*, or like *a garland wrought, and wouen with variety of flowers,* of different fmells : *Ecce odor filij mei, ficut odor agri pleni, cui benedixit Dominus.*

Caffianus Col. 9.c.7. Nilus. Gen. 27. 27.

There is yet another benefit belonging to this variety; that it procures our *Prayer* to be more eafily made by vs, and confequently that we may continue, and perfeuere longer in it. For continuall repetition of the fame thing, vfeth to make men weary; whereas variety delights, and entertaines. But that which I would fay is this. It importeth very much, towards our profitting in fpirit, that for fome tyme, we take to hart, the procuring of fome one vertue, wherof we find our felues to ftand in moft neceffity; and that principally we infift vpon that, in *Prayer*; befeeching our Lord earneft-

Tract.7.c. 3. & 9. tract. 8. c.7. Note.

earneftly, to beftow it vpon vs; and
actuating therein very often, both for
dayes, & moneths; and that we may
euer carry it before our eyes, & euen
riuetted in our harts, till we obteyne
it. For after this manner, are the buſineſſes, euen of this world, difpatched.
And fo they vfe to fay, by way of *Prouerbe* : *Lord deliuer me , from hauing to do
with a man, who hath but one buſineſſe.*

The glorious *S. Thomas* fayth, that
the Defire vfeth to be fo much ſtron-
ger, and more efficacious, as it refol-
ueth more earneftly, vpon the obteyning of fome one thing. And to this
purpofe, he bringeth that of the Prophet, *Vnam petij à domino , hanc requiram.*
One thing I haue begged of our Lord,
& the fame I will ſtil defire, *til I obteine
it.* He who pretéds to acquire any Art,
or Science, doth not ftudy one thing
to day, and another to morrow , but
he profecutes that one which he defires to learne. And fo he, who pretends
to acquire any vertue , muſt principally exercife himfelfe, for fome tyme,
therein; applying thereunto his *Prayers,*
and all his other ſpirituall Exercifes
till

S. Tho. 2.
2. q.83. ar.
14. arg. 2.

Pſa.26. 4.

Note.
S. Tho. 1.
2. q. 65.
art. 1.

till he obtayne it. Especially since (according to the doctrine of *S. Thomas*) all the morall vertues, haue great connection with one another, and they go togeather, and are interlaced in such sorte, that he who possesseth one of them, in perfectiõ, shall haue them all. And so, if you obtayne true *Humiliy*, you shall obteyne therewith, all the *vertues.* Pluck *Pride* wholy out of your hart by the rootes, and plant therein a most profound *Humility*; for if you obtayne it, you shall haue withall, much *Patience*, and much *Obedience*; and you shall complayne of nothing; and any trouble will seeme small in your sight; and all, wilbe thought too honourable and easy for you, in respect of that which you deserued. If you haue *Humility*, you will also haue much *Charity* towards your brethren, esteeming them to be all good, and only your selfe, starke naught. You will haue much *simplicity of hart,* and will not lightly passe your iudgment vpon any other; but will feele your owne miseryes, and faults so much, as that you will not thinke of other folkes.

And

And after the same manner, we might go discoursing vpon other vertues.

For this reason also, it is a very good course, to apply your particuler *Examen*, to that, which you direct your *Prayer* too, and so to ioyne one, with the other. For in this sort, all our *Exercises*, being bent one way, at once, much businesse wilbe done. And *Cassian* proceedeth yet further: For not only in our *Examen*, and the most retired kind of *Prayer*, will he haue vs insist vpon that, wherof we haue most need; but also that we should many tymes in the day, lift vp our spirit to our Lord, for that purpose, with *iaculatory Prayers*, and sighes, and groanes of our hart; and that we also shall do well, to add other pennances, & mortifications, and particuler deuotions, to the same end, as I shall shew els where, more at large. For if this be the greatest necessity which I haue, if this be the greatest Vice, or euill inclination, which raignes in me, and which makes me fall into the greatest faults; if, vpon the rooting vp, and ouercomming of this vice, and obteyning the

con-

Note.

Cassianus.

Tract.7.c. 9.

contrary vertue, dependeth the ouercoming and rooting vp of all Vice, &
the obteyning of all vertue; all diligence and labour shalbe but well imployed, in this businesse.

*Chrisost.
tract. de
oratione.*

S. Chrysostome sayth; That *Prayer is*
as a *fountaine*, in the middest of an Orchard, or Garden, without which
fountayne, all is withered and dry; but
with it, all is greene, and fresh, and
flourishing. Our soule must be watered, by this *fountaine* of *Prayer*. For this
is that, which must keepe the plants
of all vertue, in continuall freshnes &
fertility, as *Obedience, Patience, Humility,
Mortification, Recollection,* and *Silence*:

Note.

But as in a *Garden,* or *Orchard,* there
vseth to be some one tree, or dainty
flower, which is more esteemed and
regarded, & to which the *water* is conducted with more care, then to the
rest; and although water should be
wanting to others, it must not be
wanting to it; & although there want
tyme for tending the rest, there will
not want tyme for it: iustso it must be
in the *Orchard,* and *Garden* of our *soule.*
It must all be watered, and conserued,
by

by the spring of *Prayer* ; but yet still,
you are to haue an eye to some one
principall thing, wherof you are in
greatest need, and to that you must
chiefly resort; and for that, there must
neuer want any tyme. And as at the *Chap. 11,*
going out of your *Garden*, you lay
hold of that *flower* which contents you
most, and you go out with it, in your
hand; so also in *Prayer*, you are to lay
hold of that, wherof you haue most
need, and to gather it, as a *Fruite* from
thence.

Hereby sufficient answere is giuen
to that which vsually is asked: If it be
good for a man to draw that fruite
from *Prayer*, which is agreable to the
Exercise, whereupon he *meditates?* We
haue already said, that although a man
must euer haue a particuler eye, vpon
that wherof he hath most need; yet
with all, that it is good for him, to
exercise himselfe, and to actuate in the
affects and acts of other vertues, agreable to the *mystery* which is meditated.
But yet a point of great importance
is to be obserued heer; That those affects, and acts which we shall make
and

and exercise in *Prayer*, about those vertues, which occur to vs, in conformity of that which is meditated, are not to be passed ouer superficially, or cursorily; but at great leasure, & by making a quiet stād vpon them, till such tyme as we satisfy our selues; and till we feele, that it sticks, as it were, by the very ribs of our soule; and is, after a sort incorporated therunto. And this we are to do, althogh it cost vs the whole houre, as was said, before. For one of these affects, and acts continued after this sort, is much better, and doth profit vs more, then to make many acts of seuerall Vertues, and passe them ouer, in a posting manner.

One of the reasons, why some do not profit so much in *Prayer*, is because they are faulty in this point, and go leaping and skipping on the acts of seuerall vertues, saying within themselues; heere an act of *Humility* comes well in, and then they make an act of of Humility, & then away; then they thinke it is to the purpose, if they make an act of *Obedience*, and then they make an act of *Obedience*; and shortly
after

Note.

after of *Patience*; & fo they go runing,
like a Cat ouer the coales ; fo lightly,
that although there were fire, it wold
do them no hurt. Therfore when they
rife from *Prayer* , all is forgotten and
loft, and they remayne as tepide, and
vnmortifyed as before. *Doctor Auila* re-
prehendeth them , who being about
one thing in *Prayer* , as foone as any
other thing, doth offer it felfe, they inftantly giue ouer the former. And he
fayth, that vfually this is a fraude of
the diuel, who by inducing them, like
fome Pye, to skip from one branch to
another, depriues them of the *Fruit* of
their *Prayer* .

*Auila cū
75.* in *Au-
di·filia.*

I fay, it importeth much, that we deteyne our felues, in the affects & defires of vertue, till fuch tyme as our
foules be euen imbrued therewith. As
if you will actuate about contrition,
or griefe for fin, you are to ftay therein, till you find a great deteftation and
horror of fin, according to that of the
Prophet; *Iniquitatem odio habui , & abomi-
natus fum.* For this will make vs depart from *Prayer*, with firme purpofe,
rather to vndergoe a thoufand deaths,

Note.

Pfa. 118.
163.

Note.

H   then

then to commit one ſingle mortall
ſinne. And ſo doth S. *Auguſtine* note
very well, that to conceiue horrour
againſt ſome ſinnes, as *Blaſphemy, the
murthring of a mans father,* and the like,
is eaſily done; for men ſeldome fall
vpon ſuch crymes : but it is to be en-
deauoured concerning other more v-
ſuall offences, wherof the Saint affirmeth, that *Conſuetudine ipſa viluerunt : By
cuſtome men haue loſt the feare, and horror
which is fit; and therefore men eaſily fall into
them.* In the ſame manner, if you will
actuate, and exerciſe your ſelues in *Humility,* you muſt deteine your ſelues, in
the affect and deſire of being meanely
eſteemed, and deſpiſed, till at laſt your
ſoule may go drinking vp, and be imbrued with this affection, and deſire; &
ſo all theſe fumes, and frothes of pride,
may go diminiſhing, and decaying.
And the ſame is to be done, in exerci-
ſing the affects, and acts of other vertues.

Hereby it doth eaſily appeare, how
much it will help towards our good,
that we take to hart, and inſiſt, & per-
ſeuere in the demaund of ſome one
thing,

thing, after the fashiō which we haue
declared. For if this affect, and desire
of being despised, and held in meane
accounte, or any other like affect,
might continue in vs, one houre in
the morning, and another in the euening, and as much in the day following, and diuers other dayes after that; it
is plaine inough, that it wold worke
another manner of effect in our hart;
and our soules would receiue another manner of impression, and incor-
poration of that vertue, then if we
should passe it, lightly ouer. *S. Chryso-* Chryso-
stome sayth, that as no one shower of stome.
raine, nor watering by the hand, will
suffice for any soile, how fruitfull soeuer it may be, but there wilbe need of Note.
many showers, and many waterings;
so also will it be necessary, that our
soule may haue many wateringes of
much *Prayer*, to the end that it may be
bathed, and imbraed therewith. And
he bringeth, to this purpose, that of the
Prophet, *Septies in die laudem dixi tibi:* Psa. 118.
Seauen tymes a day did the *Prophet Da-* 164.
uid water his soule, with the streame
of *Prayer*; and he deteyned himselfe

much,

much, in the same affects, repeating the same, ouer and ouer, many tymes, as is to be seene abundantly in the Psalmes. And in one alone, he repeateth the same thing, seauen and twenty tymes, *Et in eternum misericordia eius*; proclairing, and exalting the mercy of our Lord. And in fiue only verses, of another Psalme, he awaketh, and inuiteth vs, to praise God, an eleauen seuerall tymes.

And Christ our Lord, did, by his owne example, instruct vs in this kind of *Prayer*; and in perseuering about the same thing, as we see in his Prayer of the *Garden*, for he was not contented to make that Prayer, to his *Eternall Father*, only once; but he renewed it the second, & the third tyme, repeating the selfe same words, *Eumdem sermonem dicens*. Yea, and the holy Gospell sayth, that at the end, he prayed more at large, then he had done before: To teach vs, that we are to insist, and perseuer in *Prayer*, about some one, and the same thing; repeating it, and replying more then once For by this meanes, and by perseue-

tance

Psal 135.
Psal. 150.

Matt. 26.
44.

Lucæ. 22.
43.

tance therein, we shall come, to attaine
that vertue, and perfection, which we
desire.

CHAP. XVI.

How we may be able to deteyne our selues
much in Prayer, about the same thing :
and the way and practise of a very profita-
ble kind of Prayer is set downe ; and that
is, to descend to particular Cases.

IT remaynes, that we deliuer the
manner which we are to hold herein; to the end that we may be able to
deteyne our selues in Prayer, a long
tyme together, in desire of one, and
the same vertue, since it is of so great
importance, as hath beene sayd. The
playne, and vsuall meanes which is
wont to be giuen for this purpose, is
to procure to continue the selfe same
act, and affect of will, or to reiterate
it, and repeate it agayne, like one who
giues a push to a wheele, that it may
not stand; or like one who still is ca-
sting fresh wood into the fire; helping our selues for this purpose, of the
same first consideration, which in

H 3   the

the beginning , did moue vs to this
affect , and defire when we finde that
it is apt to coole , and faying with the

Pfa. 114.
7.

prophet; *Conuertere anima mea in requiem
tuam , quia Dominus benefecit tibi.* Awake
thou, O my foule, and returne to thy
repofe and reft , & confider how much
it imports thee, and how great reafon
it is, that thou fhouldeft ferue our Lord,
to whome thou oweft fo much.

When the firft confideration doth
not ferue to moue vs , we muft ferue
our felues of fome other, or els paffe
on , to fome other *Point*. And for this
purpofe , we are euer to carry diuers
Points prouided; to the end that when
one of thé is difpatched, & that already
it feemes to moue vs no more, we may
proceed on to another , and yet another, which may, by refrefhing , affect, and moue vs , to what we defire.
And further we muft doe in this , as in
the cafe of corporall foode, which (to
auoyd that faftidioufnes , which is v-
fually caufed by continuing long to eat
of the fame meate) we are wont to
dreffe , and difguife in feuerall man-
ners ; and therby it feemeth new , and

Note.

giueth

giueth vs a new kind of guste. Euen
so, to the end that we may continue a
long tyme in demaund of the same
thing in *Prayer*, which is the very
food and sustenance of our soule, it is
a good way, to dresse it, in different
maners. This we may do sometymes,
by passing, from one consideration,
to another; or from one *Point* to another, as we said euen now. For euery
tyme that a man moues himselfe, and
actuates vpon the same thinge, by a
different reason, or consideration, it is
like dressing it, after another fashion, &
it growes to be like a new dish of
meate.

Againe, although there should be *Note.*
no new reason, or consideration at
hand, yet the affect and desire of the
same vertue, may, in it selfe, be dressed
seuerall wayes. As if one pretend to
get *Humility*, sometymes he may be
deteyning his minde, in the knowledge of his owne misery & weaknes;
despising and confounding himselfe
for that. At other tymes, he may enter-
tayne himself in a desire to be disestee-
med, and despised by others, not making

king any account of the opinion, and
estimation of men; but holding it all
to be meere vanity . At other tymes,
he may be giuing himselfe confusion,
and shame, to see the faults, wherin he
daily takes himselfe; and to aske both
pardon, and redresse of them, at the
hands of God. At other times, he may
do it, by admiring the goodnesse of
God, which endureth him; whereas
yet sometimes, we can hardly endure,
euen our very selues. At other tymes
by giuing him thanks, for not suffering vs to fall, into more grieuous
crymes. And by this variety, & difference of Acts, that fastidiousnes (which
vsually is caused by continuance of
the same thing) may be auoided; and
it may grow to be of facility, & guste,
to continue, and perseuer in the acts,
and affects of the same vertue, by meanes wherof, it growes to take deeper
roote, and more entire possession of the
hart. For as the *Fyle*, euery tyme that it
passeth vpon the *Iron*, carryes somewhat with it; so euery tyme that we
produce any act of *Humility*, or other
vertue, some part of the contrary vice,

is

is diminithed, and difcharged therby.

Befides this, there is another meanes to make vs perfeuere, in defire of the fame thing in **Prayer**, many daies togeather, which is both very eafy, and very profitable; and this is, by difcending to particuler cafes. The teachers of me in the way of *Spirit*, do note, that we muft not content our felues, to draw from *Prayer*, a *generall Purpofe* to ferue God; or only to proceed in vertue, and to be perfect, at large; but that we muft defcend in particuler, to that wherein we know or conceiue, that we may moft pleafe, and ferue our Lord. Neither yet, are we to content our felues with conceauing any generall defire of any particuler vertue, as namely to be *humble*, to be *obedient*, to be *patient*, or to be *mortifyed*, becaufe this kinde of defire, or rather velleity of any vertue, is intertayned thus in generall, euen by vicious men. For as *vertue* is truly beautifull, & honorable, and of great vfe, not only for the next, but euen alfo for this life; fo it is an eafy thing to loue it, and to defire it, in fuch a generall manner. But we, when

Note.

when we meditate vpon that vertue which we defire, muft difcend to particuler cafes.

As for example; if we pretend to obteyne a great *Conformity* with the will of God, we muft defcend to conforme our felues, with his will, in particuler things; afwell in ficknes, as in health; afwell in death, as in life; afwell in tentation, as in confolation. If we pretend to obteyne the vertue of *Humility*, we muft alfo defcend to particulers, by imagining fuch cafes, as may be prefented, or which vfe to offer thefelues, for our being defpifed, or difeftemed; and fo, in the reft of the Vertues. For thefe are thofe particulers, which are vfually moft felt, and wherein the difficulty of the vertue doth moft confift; and wherby a man is beft difcouered, and proued; and thefe are alfo the meanes, wherby vertue, is beft obteyned.

We muft alfo procure to begin to make our firft inftances, by thofe things, which are of the leffer forte, & more eafy; & we are afterward to rife to the more hard, wherein we thinke

we

we should haue more difficulty, if the
occasion were offered; & so to go ad-
ding somewhat, & rising vp by little,
and little, from the lesse, to the greater.
And we must actuate in the particulers, as if we had them present with vs;
& that, so long, as that nothing which
concernes the Vertue to which we
pretend, may present it selfe to vs, *to
which we may not boldly make head, and so
the field remaine ours.* And when any
reall, and true occasions do occur, we
must first imploy our selues in them,
disposing our selues to manage them
well, and with profit, euery one, according to his state. A good seruant of
God, did also add this aduise, that in
Prayer we should propound something
in particuler, concerning such, or such
a Vertue, which we should act that
day. So low as this, do they say, that
we must descend in *Prayer.*

This is one of the most profitable *Chap. 14.*
things, which we can exercise in
Prayer; for it must be *Practicall*, that is
to say, addressed to action, which may
helpe vs to worke, according to that
vertue which we desire to obtayne; &

to explane the difficultyes, & to ouercome the repugnances, which may
oppofe themfelues ; and becaufe it importeth much, that we make triall, and
take effay, as it were, of our felues, before , as fouldiers vfe to do , who before they go to the warre, vfe to try
themfelues in tiltings, and torneys, &
barriers, and incounters, and other fuch
like exercifes , that they may be the
better difpofed, and dextrous towards
a true warre. And *Caffian* doth much

Caffianus
col. 19. *c.*
16.

commend this Exercife , for the van-
quifhing of Vice, and Paffion , and for
the obteyning of Vertue. Yea, & *Plu-*

Plutarch.
Epift. ad
Pac· de
tranquill.
animi.
Seneca. l.
de confo-
latione. ad
Hefuiam
cap. 5.

tarch himfelte, and *Seneca* alfo, amongft
the *Pagans.* fay, that ignorant men do
not vnderftand how much it imports
towardes the appeafing of troubie ,
when it arriueth, to imploy the thoght
vpon it, before hand.

They fay it helpeth much , to beftow a mans thoughts in the confiderations of difficultyes , and troubles.
For that, as he who imployes his mind
vpon foft, and delightfull things, ma-

Note.

kes himfelfe effeminate, and loofe, &
good for nothing; and vpon the ap-
proach

proach of any thing which is contrary and offensiue to such a one, he receiueth much disgust; and being accustomed to that base kind of delicacy,
he turnes his backe , and seekes a lea-
ning-place for his hart, vpon certaine
agreable, and delightfull obiects; so he
who doth accustome himselfe, always
to imagine sicknes, banishment, im-
prisonment, and all those other aduersityes, which may happen, wilbe better disposed, and prouided for them,
when they come; and we shall growe
to find, that these are things which giue more feare in the beginning , then
they bring hurt in the end. *S. Gregory* *Greg.ho.*
deliuered this excellently well; *Minus* *35.super*
enim iacula feriunt, quæ præuidentur: The *Euang.*
blow wounds not so deeply , when
you were expecting it , and had halfe
swallowed it before it came , as when
it surpriseth you, vpon the sudden.

The example for this purpose is ex-
cellent,which we read of our *B. F. Ig-* *Li. 5.c.1.*
natius. When once he was sicke , the *vitæ P.N.*
Phisitian willed him that he should not *Ignatij.*
giue place to sorrow, nor to pensiue
thoughts. Vpon this occasion, he began

gan to thinke attentiuely, within himfelfe, what kind of thing might happen to him fo vnfauory, & vntoward,
as to afflict, and trouble the peace, and
reft of his foule. And hauing paffed
the eyes of his confideratiõ, ouer many
things, one only occurred, which ftuck
neerer to him then the reft, & it was,
*If perhaps the Society fhould come to be dif-
folued.* He proceeded on, to examine
himfelfe, how long the affliction, and
paine were likely to hold him , in cafe
fuch a thing as that, fhould happen.
And it feemed to him (fo that it fhould
happen, without his fault) that within
one quarter of an houre, wherein he
might recollect himfelfe, and be in
Prayer, he fhould be deliuered of that
difquiet, and fhould returne to his ac-
cuftomed tranquillity, and peace of
mind. And he yet added further, that
he would hope to holde that quiet-
neffe and tranquillity, although the *Society* fhould be diffolued, and defeated,
euen *as a graine of falt , is, in the water.*
This is a very good, and a very profitable kind of *Prayer.*

Iac, 5. 13.   The Apoftle *S. Iames ,* in his *Canonicall*

call Epistle sayth: *Tristatur aliquis vestrum,* *oret:* when you feele your selfe in affliction, or discomfort, resort to *Prayer,* and there you shall find comfort and remedy. And so did the *Prophet Dauid;* *Renuit consolari anima mea; memor fui Dei,* *& delectatus sum.* When he found himselfe discomforted, he remembred God, and raised vp his hart to him; and presently his soule was filled with this ioy and consolation; This is the wil of God, so he will haue it : which is the contentment of all contentments.

Psal. 76. 4.

Now, as after the arriuall of the occasion of trouble, it is very good & expedient, to resorte to *Prayer,* for the bearing of it well; so also doth it much importe, to take this remedy, by way of preuention, and preseruatiue, to the end that afterward, it seeme not new and hard, but gentle, & light. *S. Chrysostome* sayth, that one of the principall causes why the Holy *Iob,* continued so firme, and constant in all his aduersityes, and troubles, was, becaufe he had prouided himselfe for them, by way of imagination, and premeditation, and actuation vpon them; as vpõ

Chrys. ho. de auari-tia.

a

a thing which might happen, according to that which himfelfe relateth,

Iob. 3. 25. *Quia timor quem timebam, euenit mihi; &
quod verebar, accidit.* But now if you be
not prouided for it before had, & if euē
in the bare defire, you finde difficulty;
what will become of you, in the
worke it felfe? And if yet, whilft you
are in *Prayer*, & when you are far from
the occafion, you find not hart, and
courage inough in your felfe, to im-
biace fuch an action, and occafion, and
contempt, and trouble as is on foote;
what will become of you, when you
are gone from Prayer, and when the
difficulty of the occafion & action is
at hand? And when you are remoued
from the meditation & confideration,
of the example of Chrift our Lord,
which giues you breath, and hart?
When you are fometymes in *Prayer*,
you are carried to the defire of fuch occafions as thofe, and yet when the occafion is offered you faile; what will
Tho. de
Kempis. become of the bufines, if euen in the
tyme of *Prayer*, you defire it not? If he
who *purpofeth*, do often *faile*, how fure
will that other man be to faile, who
late,

late, or neuer will fo much as *purpofe*?

By this meanes, we giue a man very copious matter, to continue, & perfeuere in *Prayer*, concerning the fame
thing, and with the fame affect or defire, many howers togeather, & many
dayes. For the particuler cafes which
may occurre to vs, and to which we
may defcend, are without number; &
to be able to make head to all, will
finde vs worke inough, to do. And
when you fhall arriue to thinke, that
you finde ftrength inough in your
minde for all, and that you can performe it with a good will; do not yet
conceiue, that your bufineffe is already
brought to an end. You haue yet a lõg
way to go. For there is a great deale
of difference, betweene doing, and
faying; and betweene the *defire*, & the
deed. It is clere, that the *deed*, is farre
more difficult, then the *defire*. For in
the *deed*, or worke, the obiect it felfe is
prefent; but in the *defire*, there is nothing prefent, but the *imagination* of the
deed. And fo it happeneth to vs many
times, that in *Prayer*, we are full of feruour; and it feemes to vs, as if nothing

Note.

I   were

were able to ftand in our way. And yet afterward, when the occafion is offerred, and that it calls vs to put our hand to worke, we find our felues far, from what we thought.

It fufficeth not therfore, that you finde thofe good defires in your felues; but you muft procure, that they may prooue fo full of efficacy, that they may extend, or reach to the very *worke*; for this is the true touch of *Vertue*. And if you fee that your *deeds* agree not with your *defires*, but that when an occafion is offered, you difcerne your felfe to be another man, then when you were in *Prayer*; be confounded with fhame, to find that all goes away in bare *defires*. Or rather confounde your felues with fhame, becaufe thofe *defires*, by all probability, were not true ones, but conceits, and imaginations; fince fo poore, and fo weake a thing, can put you afterward into diforder & difguft; & can make you turne backe, where you were before. And as the Smith, when his worke prooues not well, returnes yet once againe to his *Auuile*, to redreffe & accommodate it, that

that it may come right; so are you to
returne to this *Anuile* of *Prayer* , that so
you may beate your *desires* into a better mould; & giue not ouer, till your
desire, and your *deed* shake hands together; and so, as that there be no more
falling out.

Yea and yet, euen when you shall
arriue to this, that you conceiue your Note.
selfe to beare the occasions which are
offered you, with vertue; do not yet
make your selfe belieue, that all the businesse is brought to an end. For in the
selfe same worke, there are many degrees, and steps, wherby to rise , before
you can arriue to the perfection of that
Vertue. For first you must exercise
your selfe to carry, with *Patience*, all
the occasions which shalbe presented;
for this is the first degree of *Vertue*. Suffer things at least with *Patience*, if you
cannot do it with *Alacrity*. And for the
performing euen of this , there wilbe
inough to do for some dayes, and not
a few. And when you shall haue arriued, to beare al hard incounters with
Patience ; yet much more way is to be
made, for the attayning to the perfe-

I 2   ction

ction of *Vertue*. For (as a Philosopher
sayth) *the signe that a man hath obteyned
the perfection of a vertue , is when he perfor-
mes the workes therof (prompte, faciliter, &
delectabiliter*) with promptitude , with
facility, and with delight. Well then,
consider if you performe the workes of
vertue, of *Humility* , of *Pouerty* of *spirit*,
of *Patience* , and of the other vertues ,
with *promptitude, with facility , and with
delight ,or gust* ; and you shall see therby, if you haue obteyned that *vertue.*
Consider if you be as glad of *dishonour,*
and *contempte* , as worldely men are
wonte to take delight , in *honor* , and
estimation: which is the *Rule* , that our

C. 4. exam.
6. 4. &
reg. 11.
Summa ij.

B. F. *Ignatius* sets before vs, he hauing
taken it first, out of the Gospell. Consider, if you be as glad, and do take as
much gust, in *pouerty* of dyet, & cloa-
thing, and lodging, and that the very
worst of the house be giuen to you,
as the couetous man would be , of
full coffers. Consider , if you be as
glad of *mortification* , and *suffering* , as
they of the world, vse to be, of *repose,*
and *rest.* If then, we be to arriue to
this perfection, in euery vertue , we
                                        shall

fhall well haue inough to do, for many dayes, and peraduenture years, although we did attempt, but fome one
of them .

Chap. XVII.

That in the confideration of thefe Myfteries,
we are to go on, at good leafure, and not to
paffe ouer them fuperficially : and of fome
meanes which help therein .

IN the confideration of diuine *myfte-*
ries , it doth alfo much importe, to
dig and found towards the fame thing,
and not to paffe curforily, through   Note?
them. For one *miftery* well confidered,
and pondered , will profit vs more,
then many, which are looked vpon
with fuperficiall eyes. Our *B. F. Igna-*   *P. N. Ig-*
tius, in his booke of *fpirituall Exercifes,*   *natius lib.*
doth therefore make fo much account   *Exercitio-*
of *repetitions,* as that inftantly after eue-   *rum fpiri-*
ry *Exercife* men are to make one *Repe-*   *tualium.*
tition, and fometymes two. For that
which a man findes not, the firft tyme,
by perfeuerance, he will find, the fe-   *Matt. 7.*
cond. *Quia qui quærit inuenit, & pulfanti*   8,
aperie-

aperietur. Moyfes ftrucke with his *rod,* vpon the *rocke,* and drew forth no *water* vpon the firft blowe ; but he drew it forth, vpon the fecond.

And Chrift our Lord, did not cure, at a clap, one of thofe blind men in the *Gofpell* ; but he went curing him, by little, and little. Firft he applyed *fpit-tle to his eyes,* and asked him if he faw any thing. The patient anfwered, that he faw certaine things in groffe, but that he diftinguifhed not well, what they were. *Video homines, velut arbores ambulantes. The men feemed to him, but walking trees.* Our Lord returned to apply his hands to his eyes, and he cured him out right ; fo that he faw diftin-ctly and cleerely. So doth it vfe to be in *Prayer,* when turning, & returning to the felfe fame thing, one difcoue-reth more, then at the firft. As when a man enters into a darke roome, at the firft he feeth nothing; if he continue a while, he begins to fee. Particulerly we muft procure to deteyne our felues ftill, in the confideration of things, till fuch tyme as we may be very well *vn-beguiled,* and fully poffeffed of what is true ;

true; and well conuinced and resolued, vpon the doing of what is fit. For
this is one of the chiefe *Fruits*, which
we are to draw out of Prayer: and
wherein it concernes vs much, to go
well grounded, as we said before. *Cap. 9.*

As for the meanes, which are to help
vs, to consider and ponder these *mysteryes* in this manner, if our Lord send
downe, some little beame of his diuine light, and open the eyes of the
soule, it findes so much to consider, and
hath so much, wherein to deteyne it
selfe, that it can say with the *Prophet, Psal. 118.*
Reuela oculos meos, & considerabo mirabilia 18.
de lege tua. Lætabor ego super eloquia tua, si-
cut qui inuenit spolia multa. The second of
these places, declares the first. I will reioyce in the consideration of those mi-
steryes and meruailes, which I haue
found in thy law, as a man would reioyce, after he had won a battell, and
met with abundance of rich spoiles.

With the blessed *S. Augustine,* and *S.*
Francis, the whole dayes & nights did
passe at ease, in the Consideration of
these two, or three words, *Nouerim*
te, & nouerim me. Let me know my selfe,

I 4   *and*

*and let me know thee. Deus meus, & omnia.
My God, and my all things.* Which is a
kinde of Prayer, of great conformity,
with that, wherof the Prophet *Isay*
sayth, that it was vsed by those Citi-
zens of Heauen, who being suspen-
ded in the *Contemplation* of that diuine
Maiesty, are perpetually singing, and
saying, and repeating, *Sanctus, Sanctus,
Sanctus; Holy, Holy, Holy.* The same, sayth
S. *Iohn*, speaking in the *Apocalyps*, of
those *Mysterious beasts, which stood before
the throne of God: Et requiem non habebant
die ac nocte, dicentia, Sanctus Sanctus, Sanctus, Dominus Deus omnipotens, qui erat, &
qui est, & qui venturus est.* And they had
no rest, nether by day, nor night, from
saying, Holy, Holy, Holy, Lord God
Omnipotent, who was, who is, and
who is to come.

But to the end that we may arriue
to this, it is fit (forasmuch as is on our
part) that we vse to deteyne our selues, in the consideration of the *mysteryes*, still pondering, and sounding into
the particularityes therof, and exercising our selues therein. *Gerson* sayth,
That one of the principall meanes which we
can

Isa. 63.

Apoc. 48.

Gerson 3
*p. alphab.
7s, litera
D. & al-
phab.* 77.
litera Z.

can set downe, and which will help vs *most, towards the enabling of* vs *to make Prayer well, wilbe, the very ordinary, & continuall Exercise therof.* It is no businesse this, which can be taught by *Rhetorick,* and *Figures*; nor is to be learned, by only hearing many discourses, nor reading many treatises of *Prayer*; but by putting the hand to worke, and by much pra-ctise therof. When a mother will teach her child to go, she spends not a whole houre in giuing him lessons, about the fashion that he is to hold in go-ing; bidding him change the posture of his feete, now in this fashion, and then in that; but by putting him vpon the exercise of it, she makes him goe; & so the child learnes, and knowes, how he is to goe.

Now this is the very meanes, wher-by we are to learne this Science of *Prayer*. And although it be very true, that for the obtayning of the guyft of *Prayer*, or any other, which is supernaturall, no labour of ours is suf-ficient, but it must come from the gra-tious, and liberall hand of God; *Quia Dominus dat sapientiam, & ex ore eius pru-*
*   dentia,*

Note:

Prou. 2.

dentia, & scientia ; because it is our Lord
who giueth wisdome, and prudence,
and science proceedeth out of his
mouth ; Yet his diuine Maiesty is pleased, that we should exercise our selues
therein, as carefully, as if we were to
obteyne it only by that meanes. For
he disposeth of all things sweetly ; *At-*
tingit à fine vsq ad finem fortiter, & disponit
omnia suauiter. And so he disposeth of
the workes of *Grace*, aswell as of the
workes of *Nature.* And as other arts &
sciences, are obteyned by practise, so is
also this of *Prayer.* By playing on the
lute, a man learnes to play ; by going,
to goe ; and by *Praying,* a man learnes to
Pray. And so *Gerson* sayth, that the
cause, why, at this day, there are so few
Contemplatiues, is through the want
of this practise. We find that anciently
in those *Monasteryes* of *Monkes*, there
were so many persons of great *Prayer,*
and *Contemplation* ; and now you shall
haue difficulty, to find a man of great
Prayer ; and when you shall speake to
men of *Cotemplation,* it seemes to them,
as if you were talking of *Metaphisicks*,
or *Morisco's*, which is not to be vnderstood.   **The**

Sap. 8. 1.

The caufe hereof is, for that anciently thofe holy *Monks* did exercife themfelues much in *Prayer*; and the young
men who entred into thofe *Monafteryes*,
were prefently tasked, and inftructed
therein, and were made to practife it
much, as we read in the rule of *S. Pa-
comius*, & other *Fathers* of thofe *Monks*.
And fo *Gerfon* giues this aduife, as very
important, for *Monafteries*, That they
are to haue amongft them, certayne
perfons of fpirit, who may be learned,
and of great practife in *Prayer*; and
who may inftruct young men from
their very entrance into *Religion*, how
they are to exercife themfelues in
Prayer. And our *B. Father*, tooke this
Counfell fo much to hart, & did leaue
it fo well recommended in the *Confti-*
tutions, that not only at the firft, in
their houfes of *Nouitiate*, there fhould
be fome to inftruct fuch as enter new-
ly; but in all the *Colledges* alfo, and *Pro-*
feſſed Houfes of the *Society*, he commaunds, that there be a Prefect ouer
fpirituall things, who may attend to
this, and obferue how euery one proceedeth in *Prayer*, for the great importance,

3i p. *Con-*
ftit. c.1.12.
& 4. p. c.
10. 7,

tance, wherof he tooke that pointe
to be.

Another thing alſo, is to help vs
much, towards our continuance in
this exerciſe of Prayer, and to perſeuer
in it much; and this is, to haue a great
loue to God, and to ſpirituall things.
And ſo ſaid the Royall Prophet; *Quo-*
modo dilexi legem tuam Domine ? tota die
meditatio mea eſt. How much, O Lord,
do I loue thy Lawe ? I am not ſatiſ-
fyed with thinking on it, all day and
night. This is my only intertainment
and delight. *Et meditabar in mandatis*
tuis quæ dilexi. So that, if we did loue
God much, we alſo would be glad to
be thinking of him day and night, and
we ſhould not want matter wherof to
thinke. Oh with how good a will,
doth the mother ſtand thinking of
that Childe of her wombe, whome
ſhe tenderly loues ? And how little
need hath ſhe of diſcourſes, or conſiderations, to comfort herſelfe, in the
thought of him? If you ſpeake but one
word of that Child, her very bowels
are inſtantly in a commotion, and the
tears of ioy, are ſtreaming downe frō
her

Pſal. 118.
97.

Pſal. 118.
47.

Note.

her eyes, without any more difcourfes, or confiderations. Do but begin to
talke to a widow of her husband de-
ceafed, whome fhe moft dearly loued,
and you fhall fee, how inftantly fhe
will figh, and weep.

Now if thefe effects can be wroght,
by this naturall kinde of loue; (why
do I fay Naturall loue?) nay if we fee
that the furious loue of fome loft and
wretched creature, doth carry him fo
abforpt, and inebriated vpon the perfon whome he loues, as that he feemes vnable, euen to thinke of any
thing els; how much more fhould
the fupernaturall Loue of that infinite
Goodneffe, and Beauty of our Lord
God, be able to produce thefe effects?
For more powerfull is *grace* , then
eyther *nature*, or *vice*. If God were all
our treafure , our hart would inftant-
ly fly vp to him : *Vbi enim eft thefaurus* *Mat.6.21.*
tuus, ibi eft & cor tuum. All the world
thinkes willingly of him, whome it *Pro.31.18.*
loues; and of that, wherein it takes delight. And therfore, the holy fcripture
fayth, *Guftauit, & vidit. Guftate & videte,* *Pfa.31.9*
quoniam fuauis eft Dominus. The *Guft*
may

may precede the *seeing* ; but the *seeing* causeth more *guste*, and more *loue*. And

S. Tho. 2. so S. Thomas speaking of this, sayth :
2. 9. 160. *That Contemplation is the daughter of Loue,*
7. ad, 1. *becauſe Loue is the roote therof.* And he also sayth, *that Loue is the end of Contem-*
plation; for by the louing of God, a man is in-
clined to thinke, and contemplate vpon him;
and how much more he contemplates, ſo much
more he loues him. For good thinges
haue this property, that when they are
seene, they inuite to loue ; & the more
we ſe them, the more we loue them;
and the more do we ioy, in continuing to see, and loue them.

CHAP. XVIII.

It is shewed after a practicall manner, how
it is in our power, to pray euer well if we
will ; and to gather Fruite *from thence.*

Cap. 4. & T H A T moſt excellent, and extra-
ſeqq. ordinary *Prayer,* wherof we ſpake
before, is a moſt particuler guifte of
God; which he imparteth, not to all,
but only to ſuch as it pleaſeth him.
But this ordinary, and playne *Mentall*
Prayer,

Prayer, wherof now we treat, our Lord denieth to none. And it is the errour of some, that because they obteyne not that other rich *Prayer*, and *Contemplation*, it seemes to them, that they cannot pray at all, and that they are not fit, for this holy exercise; whereas yet euen this, is a very good, and very profitable kind of *Prayer*, and with it we may become *perfect* . And if our Lord be pleased, to impart that other *high* Prayer vnto vs, this inferiour kind of Prayer is a very good, and a very proper disposition, for the obteyning of it. I will therefore now declare how, with the grace of our Lord, it is in our hand to make this Prayer, euer well, and to gather *Fruite* from thence, which is a matter of much comfort.

By two meanes we may very well inferre thus much, vpon that which hath beene said. The first is, because the manner of Prayer which our *B. Father* hath taught vs, is to exercise therein the *Three powers of our soule*; placing, with our *Memory*, before the eyes of our *Vnderstanding*, the *Point* or *Mistery*, vpon which we meane to make our
Prayer;

Prayer; and then to enter in, with our *Vnderstanding* it selfe, *discoursing, meditating,* and *considering* those things which may serue most for the mouing of our *Will*; and then are the affects and desires of the *Will* it selfe to follow: and this third, we haue already said, to be the chiefe part, and *Fruite*, which we are to gather from Prayer. So that Prayer, consisteth not, in that sweetnes and sensible gutte, which sometymes we feele, and do experiment within our selues; but in the acts which we make, with the *powers of our soules.* Now the doing of this, is euer in our power, though we be neuer so dry, and discomforted. For although I should be more dry then any sticke, and more hard then any stone, yet would it be in my power (with the fauour of our Lord) to make an act of detestation, and *griefe* for my sins; and an act of the *Loue* of God; and an act of *Patience*, and an act of *Humility*; and to desire to be disgraced, and despised, in imitation of Christ our Lord, who would needs be disgraced, and despised, for loue of me.

Note.

It

It muſt heere be alſo obſerued, that the buſineſſe of making good Prayer, and the *Fruite* therof, doth not conſiſt, in that one make ſo much as theſe very acts themſelues, with guſte, or ſenſible conſolation; nor in that he feele much, euen of what he is doing; nor doth the goodneſſe and perfection of the *acts* themſelues, nor the merit which followes vpon them, conſiſt in this. This I ſay, is to be noted much. For it vſeth to be an errour, very common to many, who diſcomfort themſelues, as conceauing, that they do no good in *Prayer*, becauſe they feele not ſo much actuall ſorrow for their errours, and ſins, or ſo great affection & deſire of vertue, as they would. But theſe feelings do belong to the *Senſitiue Appetite*; whereas the *Will* is a *ſpirituall Power*, and dependeth not vpon the other. And therefore there is no neceſſity, that a man ſhould feele his owne acts, in ſuch a faſhion; but it ſufficeth that they be produced by the *Will*.

And ſo the Deuines, & Saints who treat of *Contrition*, and *Griefe for ſin*, do

K thus

thus comfort their pennitents: Who
comming to make great account of
the greuiousnes of mortall sinne, are
discomforted, for not being able to
dissolue themselues in teares; nor to
feele in themselues, that sensible griefe
which they desire. For they could find
in their harts, that euen their very
bowels, might split in their bodyes,
for sorrow of their sins. And those Authors say, *That True contrition & griefe,
consisteth not in the sensitiue Appetite, but in
the Will.* Let it trouble you to haue
sinned, because sinne is the offence of
God, who is worthy to be loued a-
boue all things; for this is true *Contrition.* That other *feeling,* when our Lord
shall impart it, do you receiue it with
giuing of thanks; and when he doth
not, be not troubled, for God exacteth
not that of you. For it is euident, that
he is not to exact that of vs, which is
not in our power; and that kind of
feeling, which you would haue, is a
guste and sensible deuotion, which is
not in your power. Therfore God ex-
pecteth not that of vs, but he expe-
cteth, that which is in our power,
which

which is, the *sorrow* of our *Will*, which hath no dependance vpon that other. And the same is to be said of the acts of the *Loue of God*. Loue you God aboue al things, with your *Will*, for this is that strong and *appreciatiue Loue*, and that which God exacteth of vs. That other, is a *tender kind of loue*, which is not in our power. The same is to be said of the acts of other vertues, and of all the good purposes, which we haue.

This truth is clerely seene by the conrrary. For it is most certayne, that Note if a man do, with his will, desire, and consent to a mortall sinne, although the same man, haue no other feeling nor take no other guste therein, yet he shall sinne mortally, and shall deserue to be condemned for it, to hell. By the same reason, he whose *Will* cōsenteth, and desireth that which is good, although he haue no other guste of feeling of it, shall please almighty God, and merit heauen. Especially since God is more ready to reward vertue, then to punish vice. Nay, many tymes, these acts, are more meritorious, and more acceptable to

G od

God, when they are done, after that dry manner, without guste, or sensible consolation; because they are more pure, and more durable, & a man placeth in the more of his owne stocke, and he is at more cost (as a man may say) then when he is carried on, by sensible deuotion. And so it is a signe of more solide Vertue, and of a *Will* more firme, and faythfull, to the seruice of God. For he, who without these helpes of gustes, and spirituall consolations, doth make those acts; what would he do with them?

M. Auila.

Father *Auila* sayth very well, *That God carryeth the other man, in his armes, as if he were a Child; but this later, goes vpon his owne legs, like a man.* Blosius saith, *That they are like such as serue some Lord, at their owne charge.* And it importeth much, that we be accustomed to pray after this manner. For the most vsuall kind of *Prayer* with many, is wont to be in drinesse; those other, are extraordinary fauours. So that, as men, who goe by *Galleys* in deepe seas, when the wind comes to fayle them, do make their way by the force of *Oares*; so they who

Blosius in monil. spiritual. c. 3.

who meane to exercise themselues in *Prayer*, when the prosperous winde of the illustrations, and fauours of God, are wanting, must procure to passe on, by the *Oares* of the *Powers of their soule*, which still are helped by the fauour of the *Holy Ghost*, though not alwayes so copiously, as at some tymes.

The secōd way, we may shew thus. *Prayer*, as hath beene sayd, is not the *end*, but a *meanes* which we take for our spirituall profit, and to obteyne victory ouer our passions, and euil inclinations; that so hauing smoothed the way, and remoued all impediments, we may deliuer or selues wholy vp, into the hands of God. When those *Cataracts* were strucken downe, from the eyes of *S. Paules* soule, by that light of heauen, and that diuine voice, which said, *Ego sum Iesus quem tu persequeris*, I am Iesus whome thou persecutest; O how did he remaine, all changed in hart? how truly conuinced, and resolued, and rendred vp to the accomplishment of the will of God? *Domine quid me vis facere*? O Lord, what wilt thou haue me do? This is

Cap. 14.

A 8. 9. 5.

K 3   the

the fruite of good Prayer. And we said
before, that we muſt not content our
ſelues, with drawing certaine generall
deſires, and purpoſes out of Prayer; but
we muſt deſcend to that particuler,
wherof we haue greateſt neede; and
we muſt prepare, and prouide our ſelues, to make good vſe of thoſe occaſions, which may, and which vſe to be
offered in that preſent day, and to proceed in all things, with edification.

I ſay therfore, (applying the diſcourſe to our purpoſe) that this, by the
grace of our Lord, will euer be in our
power to do; becauſe we may ſtill be
laying hold of thoſe things, wherof
we haue moſt need. Let one of you
lay hold vpon *Humility*, another vpon
Patience, another vpon *Obedience*, another vpon *Mortification* and *Reſignation.*
And procure to go out of your Prayer,
very humble, and very well reſigned,
and indifferent, and very deſirous to
mortify, and to conforme your ſelues,
in all things, with the will of God.
And eſpecially procure, always to
draw this fruite out of Prayer, that
you may liue well that day, and with
edifi-

edific at ion of others, euery one according to his estate. And so you shall
haue made your Prayer excellently
well; yea and better, then if you had
shed many tears, and enioyed much
consolation.

So that we are not to put our
selues in payne, for not being able to
vse much discourse, or many considerations, nor to haue other feelings and
deuotions; because *Prayer*, doth not
consist in this, but in the rest. Neither
yet are we to make much account of
those *distractions*, and flying thoughts,
which vse to disquiet vs in *Prayer*,
against our will; wherof yet we do
ordinarily complaine. When you reflect and obserue, that you are *distra-* Note.
cted, lay present hold agayne, vpon
your matter, and vpon the Fruite,
which you are to gather; and therby
you shall supply, and reuerse the losse
of tyme, which you haue made by
that *distraction*; and you shall reuenge
your selues on the Diuell, who hath
procured to diuert you, by impertinent thoughts. This is a very profitable aduise for *Prayer*. And, as when a
man,

man, who was trauelling with others,
laid himselfe downe to sleepe, & his
Camerado's passed on; but when he
awaked, he made so much haste to
ouertake them, that in a quarter of an
hower, he dispatched that way, which
he was to haue made in a whole one,
if he had not fallen asleepe : so when
you reflect, and returne to your selues, from your *distraction*, in the last
quarter of an hower, you are to carry
Chap.14. the matter so well, as to do therein, all
that which you were to haue done in
the whole hower, if you had continued in attention.

Enter presently into account with
your selfe and say, *What did I pretend to
negotiate with Almighty God , in this
Prayer? what was the Fruite, which I had
prepared to gather thence?* Humility? In-
differency? Resignation? Conformity
with the will of God ? *Well yet, I will*
Note. *not faile to fetch this Fruite , out of this
Prayer, in despite of the Diuell.* And when
perhaps you find, that euen the whole
Prayer hath gone amisse, and that you
haue not gathered the *Fruite* which
you desired, you must procure to do
it,

it, in the *Examen of your Prayer*, wherof Chap. 27.
we will fpeake afterward; and therby
you are to fupply, for the faults which
you haue made in the *Prayer* it felfe, &
fo you fhall euer gather *Fruite* therby.

Chap. XIX.

*Of fome eafy meanes, or wayes, wherby we
may haue profitable, and good* Prayer.

THERE are alfo other very eafy
wayes, which will helpe vs
much, towards the hauing of good
Prayer; wherby alfo it will appeare,
that it is euer, in our power to haue
good, and profitable *Prayer*; and that
all, are capable of *Mentall Prayer*, and
that there is none, who may not
vfe it.

As for the firft, it is very good to
this purpofe, which is aduifed by fome
Maifters of Spirit, who fay, That we
muft not make our Prayer to be a matter of fiction, or art; but we muft do
in that, as men do in bufineffe of importance, who pawfe to thinke what
they are about; and how their bufineffe

nesse speeds, and how it may be better done. So the seruant of God, is

Note

playnly, and without tricks, to deale
with himselfe, in point of Prayer, &
to say, *How goes the busineße forward of*
the spirituall profit, and of the saluation of
my soule? For this is our *busineße,* and
we are not continuing in this life, for
any other true reason, but only to negotiate this affaire. Let therefore the
religious man especially, enter into account with himselfe, & let him thinke
thus, at great leasure. *How goes my soule*
on in this busineße? What fruite haue I ga-
thered in these ten, twenty, thirty, or fourty
years, that I haue beene in Religion? What is
that, which I haue gained, or acquired in the
vertue of Humility, or Mortification? I will
see how the accounts do stand; and what I
can answere to God, for all those so great
meanes, and helpes, which I haue had in Re-
ligion, wherewith to thriue, and increase the
Principall, and Talent, which he gaue me.
And if hitherto I haue ill imployed my time,
and not knowen how to serue my selfe ther-
of, I will remedy the fault from henceforth;
and certainly, my whole life shall not paße
hereafter, as a great part therof, hath done hi-
therto.   In

In the same manner ought euery
one in his condition, with great play-
nenesse and simplicity, and without
all disguise, make a pawse to thinke in
particuler, how it goes with him, in
his place and duty; how he shalbe able
to discharge it well, and according to
the will of God; how he may carry his
businesse like a good Christian, and
gouerne his house and family, in such
sort, as that all of it, may serue God.
How he may make right vse, & beare
those difficulties with patience, which
his condition, or office carry with it.
In this, he will find inough to la-
ment, and to amend. And this wilbe
a very good, and a very profitable
kind of *Prayer*.

Iohn Gerson telleth of a seruant of
God, who was wonte to say thus,
many tymes. *It is now fourty yeare since* I
haue frequented prayer, with all care I could,
and I *neuer found a better, nor a more briefe,*
and compendious meanes, towards the ma-
king of good Prayer, *then to present my selfe,*
in the presence of God, like an infant, or
like some poore blinde, naked, and abandoned
beggar. We see that the Prophet *Dauid,*

Guliel.
Parif.

did

did vſe this kind of Prayer very often, calling himſelfe ſometymes *a ſicke man*, at other tymes an *orphane*, at other tymes a *blindeman*; and at others, *a poore Creature*, and *a beggar*. And of this, the Pſalmes are full. And we know by experience, that many, who haue vſed, and frequented this kinde of Prayer, haue come, by this meanes, to be indued with very high *Contemplation*. Do you therfore vſe it; and our Lord wilbe pleaſed, that by this meanes, you ſhall obteyne, what you deſire.

Note.

Gerſon de monte contemplat.

The Prayer of the *Beggar*, is a very good Prayer. Conſider, ſayth *Gerſon*, with how great humility and patience the poore man ſtands expecting a litle almes, at the rich mans doore; and with what diligence he goes, where he knowes, there is any almes to be giuen. And as this poore and naked, forſakē creature, ſtands before the richman, asking him almes, and hoping for the remedy of his neceſſity, with great humility, and reuerence; ſo are we to place our ſelues, before God in Prayer, repreſenting to him our *Pouerty,*

werty, our neceffity, and our mifery; &
hoping for fome remedy therof, at the
hands of his liberality and bounty. *Si-* *Pfa.* 112. 2.
cut oculi ancillæ in manibus Dominæ fuæ, ita
oculi nostri, ad Dominũ Deum nostrum, do-
nec mifereatur nostri. As the eyes of the
flaue, ftand hanging vpon the hands
of her Lord, expecting what he will
beftow vpon her; fo are our eyes to be
hanging & depending vpon our Lord
God, till fuch tyme, as we may obteyne mercy of him.

We find in that ftory, which is recounted of the Abbot *Paphnutius*,
who liued in the moft inward part of
the defert, how that hauing heard of *Pratum*
that loofe woman *Thais*, that fhe was *fpiritual.*
the fnare and perdition of many fou-
les, and the caufe alfo of many quar-
rels, and the death of many; he did
with defire to conuert her, and drawe
her to God, take the habit of a fecular
man, and money, and he went to the
Citty, where fhe dwelt, and conuerted her. And he tooke the occafion,
from fome words of hers, when (he
feeming to defire, that fhe would al-
low him fome more priuate place)
fhe

she said, *Thou art safe inough heere, from the eyes of men, who cannot see the heere; From the eyes of God, indeed, thou canst not hide thy selfe, how secret soeuer the place may be.* The story is large; but to come to that which makes to our purpose.

The woman being conuerted, he conducted her to the wildernesse, and did shut her vp into a cell; and made it fast with a seale of leade, leauing only an ouerture, in a very little window which there was, to the end that daily they might therby, giue her a little bread, and water. And *Paphnutius,* leauing her, she asked him only, how she was to pray to God. To this, the holy *Abbot* answered: *Thou doest not deserue to take the Name of God into that impure mouth of thine, but the manner of thy Prayer shalbe this: Thou shalt put thy selfe vpon thy knees; and thou shalt turne thy selfe towards the East; and thou shalt repeat these words many tymes, Qui plasmasti me, miserere mei;* O thou who madest me, haue mercy on me. In this manner she continued three years, without euer presuming to take the name of God into her mouth; but alwayes
                              carrying

carrying her many grieuous finnes before her fight, and demaunding mercy and pardon for them of our Lord, in thofe words which the Saint had taught her.

And this Prayer, was fo acceptable to Almighty God, that the *Abbot Paphnutius*, demaunding of the bleffed *Saint Anthony*, at the end of thofe three yeares, if he thought that God had pardoned her finners; *S. Anthony* called his Monks about him, and required them, that euery one fhould remaine all the next night following by himfelfe, in *Watching* and *Prayer*; to the end that our Lord might declare that to fome one of them, which was demaunded by *Paphnutius*. Being therfore all, in Prayer, *Paul* the *monke*, who was the chiefe amongft the difciples of *S. Anthony*, had a vifion of a bed in heauen, adorned with moft pretious furniture, and which was attended by foure virgins. As foone as he faw fo rich an obiect, he inftantly faid within himfelfe : This grace and fauour cannot be referued for any other, then for my father *S. Anthony*. As he was in thefe

thoughts,

thoughts, a voice defcended from heauen, and faid, *This bed of glory, is not pre-*
pared for thy Father Anthony, but for Thais
the finner. And fifteene dayes after, our
Lord was pleafed to carry her to enioy that glory, or celeftiall bed of ftate.
Do you the while, content your felues, with making this *Prayer,* & know
that you deferue to make no other.
And perhaps you may pleafe God
more by this, then if you made that
other, which you imagine.

In a certayne fpirituall Difcourfe
which is a manufcript, made by a religious *Monke* of the *Carthufians,* concerning *fpirituall Communion* , he recounteth a certayne paffage of our *B.*
F. Ignatius, and his companions, which
he affirmeth himfelfe to haue vnder-
ftood, from a perfon worthy to haue
beene belieued. How that, whilft
they were trauelling as they vfed to
do on foote, with their little bags, and
fuch like neceffaryes, vnder their armes; and going towards *Barcelona,*
there was a good honeft man, trauelling alfo in the fame way, who faw
them, and tooke pitty of them, & be-
                                    fought

fought them, with great inſtance, that
they would giue him their little bags;
ſaying that he was luſty, and ſtrong,
and would carry them well. And although they refuſed to do ſo, yet at
laſt, being importuned, they were
content; and ſo, went on, their way,
all together. Whē they arriued at their
lodging, the *Fathers*, euery one of
them, did procure to find out his corner, to recollect, and commend himſelfe to God, in *Prayer*. That other ho-
neſt man, ſeeing thē do ſo, did procure a corner alſo for himſelfe, and
caſt himſelfe downe vpon his knees,
like them. And proceeding afterward
in their way, they asked him once :
*Brother, what do you vſe to do, in that corner
of yours?* He anſwered. *That which I do, is
to ſay, O Lord theſe men are ſaints, and I am
but their beaſt. Looke what they do, and that
will I alſo do. And this* (ſayth he) *am I offering vp to God.* And the Story further
ſayth that the good man did profit ſo
much, by meanes of this *Prayer*, that
he grew to be a very ſpirituall perſon, and to be of *high Prayer*, afterward. Now who is he, that cannot vſe

L   this

this forme of *Prayer*, if he will?

My felfe did know a very ancient *Father* of the *Society* of *Iefus*, and a very great Preacher, whofe *Prayer*, for a long tyme, was to fay, with much humility, and fimplicity, to Almighty God : *O Lord, I am but a beaft, and know not how to vfe Prayer, do thou teach it me; O Lord.* With this he profited much, &

Pfal. 72.23 grew to haue moſt *high Prayer* ; that of the Prophet, being accomplifhed in him, *Vt iumentum factus fum, & ego femper tecum.* Do you therfore humble your felues, & become, in the fight of God, as if you were but poore beafts, and our Lord wilbe with you. It doth much import in the fight of God, that one do humble himfelfe ; for great matters are negotiated, and obteyned in this manner, at the hands of his diuine Maiefty. And heere the Saints do note a thing of much importáce; That

Note. as *Humility* is the meanes to obteyne *Prayer*, fo *Prayer* muſt be the meanes to obteyne *Humility*, and to go increafing in it.

And fo they fay, that when a man hath made good *Prayer*, he euer goes a
way

way much humbled and confounded.
Whereupon it followes, that when a
man parteth well contented from his
Prayer, with I know not what kind
of vaine complacence, & a close kind
of estimation, and reputation of himselfe;conceiuing,forsooth,that he hath
profitted much, and that already he is
growing a kind of spirituall man, that
Prayer deserues to be suspected. And
therfore,if you say that you are not a-
ble to draw many considerations out
of *Prayer* , nor to haue any high *Contemplations,* let your course, be to humble your selfe , and gather that *Fruite*
from your *Prayer* , and you can haue
no excuse, for not doing that ; & euen
that wilbe a very good Prayer.

It is also a very good meanes, when
a man is not able to enter *Prayer* , and
that he is in conflict with many
thoughts, and temptations, to do that
which Father *Auila* doth thus aduise,
in one of his letters: *Cast your selues at
the feete of Christ our Lord, and say; O Lord
forasmuch as this distraction, and difficulty
in Prayer,proceeds from any fault of mine, I
am hartily sory for it;but forasmuch as is*

L 2 *therein,*

Greg.l. 2.
in Ezech.
hom. 17.
*Chrysost.
ho.* 4. *de
poen. to.* 5.

*M. Auila
l.* 2. *Epist.*

Note.

therein, of thy will, and of thy punisment, I haue iustly deserued it , for my great sinnes past. And for my great negligence and errours present, I do accept it with a very good will, and I am glad to receiue from thy holy hand , this crosse, this drynesse, this distraction, this discomfort , and this spirituall desolation. This *Patience*, and this *Humility*, wilbe a very good Prayer , and will please God more , then the Prayer which you desired to haue, as we shall afterwards shew more at large.

It is written of our Father *Franciscus de Boria* , how when it seemed to him, that he had not had good Prayer, that day did he procure to mortify himselfe more, and to goe with more care, and diligence in all his workes, therby to supply the fault of his Prayer ; and so he Counselleth vs to do. This is a very good meanes to supply the fault of Prayer, yea & it wilbe also a good meanes to make our Prayer good. *S. Nilus* the *Abbot*, speaking of Prayer sayth, That as when we disorder, and discompose our selues in the day, it seemes that presently we shall feele the punishment of it in our

Prayer,

Tract. 8.
cap. 26.

P. Fran.de
Borgia.

Note.

Prayer, for there, God sheweth vs some hard countenance : so on the other side, when we haue mortifyed, and ouercome our selues, in things of difficulty, we do instantly also find it in our Prayer; for our Lord is pleased to reward vs, with ready payment. *Quidquid durum & asperum patienter tolerabis, fructum laboris, tempore orationis reperies.*

The Saint doth therupon, giue a very good aduise, for the hauing of good Prayer, and of very good conformity, with that which we haue already said. *Si orare desideras, nihil facias eorum, quæ orationi aduersantur, vt tibi appropinquet Deus, & tecum ambulet.* If you desire to haue good Prayer, do nothing which may be contrary to Prayer, and by this meanes God will communicate himselfe to you, and do you many fauours.

Nilus de oratione c. 17. & 62. in biblio. sanctorum Patrum, tom. 3.

And generally, let all men vnderstand, that the principall care which the seruant of God ought to haue, is to cleanse and mortify his hart, and to keepe himselfe free from all sinne, and to be very firme and resolute, not to

Note.

L 3 com-

commit one mortall sinne , for the whole world. Herein he is to ground himselfe well, whilest he is in Prayer and to insist and actuate vpon it , very often ; for we haue need to do so, as long as we are in this miserable life . And vpon this foundation , euery mā may build asmuch perfectiō as he will. And therfore he hath no reason to go vp and downe with complaints, but to be very gratefull to God , although he giue him no other kind, of higher Prayer. For Sanctity, consisteth not in hauing to guift of Prayer, but in do-ing the will of God. *Deum time, & mā-data eius obserua : hoc est enim omnis homo.* With this saying , *Salomon* concludeth that high sermon of *Ecclesiastes* . *Feare God and keep his Commaundements , for all man is but this.* That is to say : *In this cō-sisteth all the felicity of man ; and by this he complyeth with all his obligations; and with this, he may be holy, and perfect.*

Eccl.12.13.

Note.

I will conclude, with assigning a meanes for good Prayer, which shalbe of much comfort for all men. When you do not find in your Prayer, that ease , that attention , and deuotion, & that

internall vnion which you wish, exercise your selues , in hauing a great inclination and desire to it; & with this
you shall supply that which you conceiue to be wanting to you . For our
Lord God (as the Saints affirme) is no
lesse content, and satisfyed, with that
good desire , and will of yours, then
he would be with your high, and sublyme Prayer. *Deus , non minùs voluntate*
sanctog̃, desiderio lætatur ,quàm si tota anima
amore liquefacta, pienè sibi iungeretur. This
helpe , God taught to the holy virgin
Gertrude, and it is related by *Blosius.* He
sayth , that the Saint complayning of
her wants , and that she could not in
in Prayer, rayse her hart so high, as she
desired , and as she thought she was o-
bliged, she was taught from heauen ,
that with God it was sufficient , if the
man did indeed desire, and wish , that
he had a great desire of it , when yet
perhaps she feeled very little, or no desire at all. For iust so great , is a good
desire esteemed to be , in the sight of
God , as the mã , would fayne haue it
great. And he saith: *That in a hart which*
hath such a desire (that is to say) *which hath*

L 4   *a de-*

F.*Barth. de*
los mart y-
ris Arche-
Bracharē-
sis in suo
compendio
spirituali
c. 19. *fol,*
250*.*

Blosiu eo.
2. *dem onsi-*
lis spir itu-
al .

a desire, and will, to haue this desire, God dwelleth with a better will, then a man would be glad to stay, amongst fresh, and odoriferous flowers.

God hath no need of your high Praier, he desirs nothing but your hart; to that he lookes, and he receyues the *desires* thereof, for *deeds*. And so, agreably to this, it wilbe a very good deuotion, and a very profitable consideration, when we find our selues tepide & dry in Prayer, to consider how many seruants of God there are in Prayer ouer the world, at the very same tyme perhaps shedding tears, and peraduenture bloud, and we may imagine our selues, to be with them; and not only with them, but euen with the Angells, & other celestiall spirits, louing & praising God. And we may remit our selues to that which they do; & supply therby, the want of that which we cánot do our selues; repeating many times with our harts, and with our mouthes, those words: *Cum quibus, & nostras voces, vt admitti iubeas deprecamur, supplici confessione dicentes, Sanctus, Sanctus, Sanctus &c.* O Lord that which they
say,

Note.

say, I say; and that which they do, I
would faine do ; & iust as they praise
and loue, so would I fayne blesse, and
prayse, and loue thee. And sometymes it wilbe also good, that we remit
our selues , euen to our selues , as we
were at some former tyme, when we
conceiue our selues to haue beene in
good *Prayer*, saying : *O my Lord, that
which I did then , and as then I offered my
selfe wholy to thee, so do I offer my selfe now:
and as then I grieued for my sins, so do I
grieue now; and as then I desired Humility,
Patience, and Obedience, in the same manner, O Lord, do I craue , and beg it of thee
now.*

But aboue all, it is a most singular
good practise , to vnite our workes
with those of Christ our Lord, and to
supply our faults & imperfections by
the merits of his most sacred *Passion;*aswell in that which concerneth our
*Prayer,*as in our other actions;offering
to the eternall Father, our *Prayers,* in
vnion of the loue and feruour, wherewith Christ our Lord did pray to
him,and praise him here on earth;and
our *Fasts,*in vniō of those *Fasts,* which
                                        he

he made, beseeching him that he wilbe
pleased to supply our *Impatience*, with
the *Patience* of Christ our Lord ; our
pride with his *Humility*; and our *Malice*,
with his *Innocency*. This practise (as
Blosius relateth) was reuealed by our
Lord to some deare seruants of his, to
the end, that we may so make our
workes of much worth, and merit, &
relieue our pouerty, by his meanes;
through the infinite treasure, of the
merits of Christ our Lord.

Blosius c.
9. inslitut.
spiritual.

Chap. XX.

That we must content our selues with this
Prayer, wherof we haue spoken; and not
goe with complaint, and griefe, for not
being able to obtayne that other Prayer,
which is more high .

ALBERTVS *Magnus* sayth, that
the true humble man, doth not
presume to lift vp his hart, to a desire
of that high and rich *Prayer*, and of
those extraordinary fauours, which
our Lord doth vse, sometymes, to cō-
municate to his deare seruants. For he
estee-

Albertus
magnus de
adhærendo
Deo.

Note.

efteemeth fo little of himfelfe, that he holdeth himfelfe vnworthy of all fa- uour, and fpirituall confolation. And if at any tyme, without any defire of his, our Lord do vifite him, with any comfort; he receiueth it with feare, ac- knowledging that he deferueth not thofe vifitations; and that he knowes not, how to profit by them, as he ought. And if we had true *Humility,* we would content our felues, with any of thofe kinds of Prayer, wherof we fpake. Nay rather, we fhould hold it for a particuler fauour of our Lord, that he leades vs, by the way of *Humi- lity.* For therby, we fhall conferue our felues; and by that other way, we might perhaps, growe light-headed, and fo be loft.

S. *Bernard* fayth, that God doth car- ry himfelfe towards vs, as the Fathers of this world do, towards their little children. That when the Childe as- keth bread, they giue it him with a good will; but when the Child af- keth for a knife, wherewith to cut his bread, they will not giue it him; be- caufe they fee it is not neceffary, and that

Bern. fer s. *quadrag.*

Note.

that perhaps, it might do him hurt, by
cutting his fingers. But the father takes
the knife, and cuts the bread, that so
the child may neither be put to any
trouble, nor made subiect to any danger. In this forte doth our Lord proceed. He giues you the bread, already
cut; and will not giue you those gusts,
and consolations, which are in that
most high *Prayer*; because perhaps, you
would cut your selues; & they would
do you hurt, by making you wanton,
and guiddy, and to hold your selues
for spirituall persons, and to prefer
your selues before others. Our Lord
doth you a greater fauour, in giuing
you the *bread* already cut, then if he
gaue you the *knife*, wherewith to cut
it. If God, with your *Prayer*, giue you
a great resolution, and strength, rather
to dy, then to commit finne; and if he
keepe you, through the whole courfe
of your life, without committing a
mortall finne, what better *Prayer*, and
what better *Fruite* can you desire, then
this?

This is that answere, which the *Father* of the *Prodigall Sonne* gaue to his *el-
der*

der brother. Who seing that the *Younger*
was receiued with so much feasting
and ioy, was deepely offended with
it, and already was refusing to enter
into his *Fathers* house, saying to this
effect; *So many years are now past , since I
serue you , and haue euer beene subiect to
your commaundements , and obsequious to
your person, and you haue neuer bestowed
vpon me, so much as a Kid, to the end that I
might make merry with my friends. And as
for that other ,who hath dissipated your state,
and beene disobedient to your selfe, you haue
killed the fat calfe , and made him a sumptuous banquet, with great musique, and ioy.*
The Father makes this answere. *Fili,tu* **Luc. 15.**
semper mecum es. My sonne, know that **11.**
I do not this , as louing the other,
more then you : *You are euer remaining
in my house, and with my person. It will also
be reason, that you know and esteeme wor-
thily,of that which I do for you. Is it perhaps
a small grace and fauour, which I do you, in
continuing you euer, about my selfe ?*

The same I say in your case. Doth
it seeme a trifle, for our Lord to keepe
you euer with himselfe, and in his
house? It is a greater matter, for our
Lord,

Lord to giue you the guift of perfeuerance, and to keepe you, from euer
parting from him, and falling into
fin; then if, after you were fallen, he
fhould lend you his hand, as he did to
the *Prodigall Sonne.* It is more for him,
to keepe you, from breaking your
head, then if he fhould heale it, when
it were broken. If then our Lord, with
this *Prayer* which you haue, do giue
you this, of what can you complayne?
If with this *Prayer*, he giue you great
promptitude towards al things which
concerne his feruice, and great indif-
ferency, with intiere refignation towards all the orders of *Obedience*,
what can you defire more? If with this
Prayer, God conferue you in *Humility*,
and in his feare, and in walking wa-
rily, and in preferuing your felues
from occafions, & out of the dangers
of finne, what reafon haue you to figh
for more? This is that *Fruite* which
you were to gather out of *Prayer*, if it
were neuer fo high and fublyme. And
when, our Lord were pleafed, to giue
you many gufts and comforts in it, to
this end you were to addreffe the all.

Now

Now this is that, which God doth worke in this playne, and ordinary Prayer. He giueth you the end, and the *Fruite*, without those extraordinary meanes of eleuations, and gusts, and confolations; as they find by experience, who perseuere in it. And therfore we are to giue, for this, double thanks to our Lord. For, on the one side, he frees vs from the danger of vanity, and pride, which we might be subiect to; and on the other side, he giues vs that *Fruite*, and profit of Prayer, which is most complete. The holy Scripture faith, of the holy Patriarch *Ioseph, That he spake to his brethren, with hard, and sharpe words; and yet with all that he filled their sacks, full of corne; and commaunded his Steward, to treat them well.* Gen. 42.7. & 25. And so doth our Lord carry himfelfe many tymes towards vs.

We will neuer vnderstand, as we ought, wherein Prayer, doth indeed confist. Or to speake more properly, we will neuer vnderstand, as we ought, wherein our spirituall profit & perfection doth confist, which is the *End* and *Fruite*, to which our Prayer is ordey-

ordeyned. And ſo, many tymes, when
it goes ill with vs , we thinke it goes
well; and when indeed it goeth well,
we are apt to thinke, that it goeth ill.
Drawe you, out of Prayer, that which
we haue ſaid ; and eſpecially to proceed well that preſent day, and with

edification, as was touched before; and
you ſhall haue made good Prayer;
though whilſt you were praying, you
were as dry as a ſticke, and as hard as a
ſtone. And if you gaine not this, you
haue not made good *Prayer* , though
you were ſtreaming downe teares, all
the while , and although you had
beene eleuated vp, to the third heauen.

Henceforward therfore , do not
complayne of *Prayer* , but turne your
complaints againſt your ſelues , and
ſay, *It goes ill with me, in point of Mortifi-*

cation. It goes ill with me in point of Hu-
mility ; in point of Patience ; in point of Si-
lence, and Recollection. This indeed, is a
iuſt complaynt , becauſe it is to complayne againſt your ſelues ; for you do
not that which you ought , and yet it
is in your owne power. But that o-
ther courſe , of going , in complaynt
                                                    againſt

againſt Prayer, ſeemes to be a kinde of complayning againſt God, becauſe he giues not that kinde of way , and quietnes, and comfort , which you could deſire. This I ſay , is no good complainte. *It is no word, this , which may induce our Lord to mercy , but rather prouoke him , to wrath , and indignation,* as the holy *Iudith,* ſaid to them of *Be-thulia. Non eſt iſte ſermo, qui miſericordiam prouocet, ſed potius qui iram excitet, & furo-rem accendat.* And it is worth the con-ſidering, how contrary we are in this, to reaſon. For I find not, that we com-playne of not being willing to mor-tify, nor humble, nor améd our ſelues; which yet is the thing that we haue in our power. But we go complay-ning of that , which is not in our power , but runns vpon the accounte of Almighty God. Endeauour you to mortify, and ouercome your ſelues, & herein do that, which belongs to you, and truſt God with that which be-longs to him. For more deſire hath he, of our good, then we our ſelues. And if we do that which belongs to vs, we may reſt ſecure inough, that , for

Iudith 8. 11.

Notes

M   his

Tract.8.
Ca.24. &
seqq. &
Vide supra
Cap.5. ad
finem ex
Bernardo.

his part, he will not be wanting, to
giue vs that which is fit for vs. We will
speake more largly of this pointe,
when we treate of *Conformity with the*
will of God; where we will procure to
giue more expresse satisfaction, to this
complaint, and temptation.

CHAP. XXI.

Of the causes of Distraction in Prayer, and
of the Remedies.

THIS is wonte to be a very ordinary complaint, and therfore
the *Saints* do generally treate therof,
and especially *Cassian*. They say, that
distraction in Prayer, may rise from one
of three causes. The first, our owne
carelessnesse, or negligence; because
we go scattered in our owne thoghts,
and we set little guard vpon our hart;
and make little recolection of our senses. He who liueth in this manner,
hath no reason to wonder, how he
comes to be be *distracted* in *Prayer*, and
why he can make no way in it. For it
is cleere, that the *images*, and *figures*, and
repre-

Cassianus
collat. in
8.7.

Note.

representations of those things which he suffers to enter in, are to disquiet and molest him afterwards in *Prayer.*

The Abbot *Moyses* sayth well, *That although it is not in the power of a man to keepe himselfe from being surprised with thoughts, yet, that it is in his power, eyther not to admit the, or els to driue them away.* And he addeth further, *that it is in great part in our power to correct and mend the quality of those thoughts;* and to cause that they may be holy, & good, & that those others which are impertinent, & vayne, may grow by little & little to be forgotte. For if he giue himselfe to the spirituall Exercises of *Reading, Meditation,* and *Prayer;* if he imploy himselfe vpon good and holy workes, he wilbe sure to haue good, and holy thoughts. But if, when he spends the day, he do but feed his senses with vaine, and impertinent things; his thoughts will not faile to be of the same quality. *Collat. 1.*

To this purpose he bringeth a comparison, and it is also brought by Saint *Anselme,* and S. *Bernard.* These Saints affirme, that the hart of man is like a *Milstone,* which is euer mouing; but it is *Collat. 1. cap. 18.*

Notæ.

M 2   in

in the hand of the *Miller*, who rules it, to choose whether it shall *grinde* wheate, or oates, or any other graine ; for that which they cast before it, it will grinde. And so the hart of man, cannot be without thinking vpon somewhat, which it will grinde; but by your industry, and diligence, you may make it grind what corne you will, wheat, or rye, yea or earth it selfe; for in fine, whatsoeuer you cast before it, that will it grinde. In conformity therfore of this, if you meane to be recolected in *Prayer*, you must procure, as you conuerse, to carry you hart recollected, and to keep the gates of your senses close. For our Lord takes pleasure to treat with soules, which are, as *Gardens shut.*

And so, it was a common saying of those ancient Fathers, and it is alledged by *Cassian*. *Quales orantes volumus inueniri, tales nos, ante orationis tempus, preparare debemus; ex præcedenti enim stata, mens atque animus, in supplicatione formatur.* We must go backe againe, to begin our course, and procure to be, when we are out of *Prayer*, such as in

Prayer

Cassianus collat. 9. Abbatis Isaac.c.1. 2.

Note.

Prayer we defire to be. For of the fame
ftate and temper, which the hart fhall
haue out of Prayer, the fame it will alfo haue in Prayer. *Qualis liquor vaſi in-
funditur, taliter redolebit; & quales herbas in
horto cordis tui plantaueris, talia ſemina ger-
minabunt,* fayth *S. Bonauenture.* Such as
the liquour is, which you powre into the veſſell, fuch wilbe the fmell; &
fuch as the hearbs fhalbe, which you
plant in the garden of your hart, fuch
will the fruite, and feed be, which is
produced therby.

And becauſe it is an vfuall, and naturall thing, for a man to thinke much
of that, which he loues; if you defire
to keepe your harte firme, and ftable
in tyme of Prayer, and that your
thoughts of vayne, and impertinent
things, may growe into obliuion, and
to an end; you muft mortify your loue
therof, defpifing all earthly things, &
you muft lodge your hartes in heauen.
And how much the more you fhall
profit, and increaſe in this; fo much the
more fhall you increaſe, and profit in
ftability, attention, and deuotion in
Prayer.

*Bonauent.
de profe-
ctu, reli-
gioſi li. 2 c.*
58.

M 3   Se

Secondly, *Distraction* vseth to grow, from the temptations of our enemy the Diuell. *S. Basil* sayth, That the diuell, seing our Prayer to be the meanes wherby all good cōmeth to vs, procures by all wayes possible, to hinder vs, and diuert vs therein; to the end, that, hauing depriued vs of this succour, he may the more easily find entrance into our soules, for his temptations and deceits. He carrieth himselfe towards vs, as the Captaine of *Holofernes* did, for the taking of the Citty of *Bethulia*, which defended it selfe against him. For he *brake the Conduites wherby water was conueyed vnto the Citty*. And so the diuell doth procure, with all diligence, to disorder, and breake in vs, this *Aqueduct* of Prayer, wherby the water of grace, and of all spirituall good is deriued into our soules. And *S. John Climacus* sayth, that as vpon the ringing of the bell, Faythfull Christians and *Religious men*, do visibly assemble themselues to make Prayer, & to praise our Lord; so our enemyes who are the diuells, do also associate themselues inuisibly, to tempt, & hinder vs from Prayer.   In

Basil. ser de renunciatione saeculi & spiritt. nerfect. Cassian l. 10. cap. 10. & Nilus 44 & 47. de oratione.

Note.

Iudith 7. 6.

Climacus gra. 18.

In the *Pratum spirituale*, it is re- *De Ab-*
counted of one of thofe Fathers of the *bat. Mar-*
defert, that rifing one night to Prayer, *cell.*
and finging of *Pfalmes*, as his cuftome
was, he heard the found of a trumpet,
which was like the figne of giuing a
battell. And the holy old man being
troubled at it, and wondring from
whence that noife might come, into
fo follitary a place, where there was
no war, nor no fouldiers; the Diuell
appeared to him, and faid, that although he thought that there was no
battell towards, yet indeed there was;
and that the trumpet fhewed that the
diuells were about to begin it, againft
the feruants of God; and that if he defired to be free from it, he fhould returne to take his reft, and if not, that
he was to looke to himfelfe. But he,
confiding in our Lord, did enter into
his Prayer, and continued in it.

One of the things wherby the excellency, and great importance of
Prayer may be particulerly well def-
cerned, is the watchfull and curft eye
which the diuell carrieth towards it;
and the continuall warre, which he

M 4 makes

Nilus ca.
44. & 47.
de oratio-
ne. & ca.
100 &
seqq. refer.
aliqua
Exempla
circa hoc
in biblio.
Sancto-
rum PP.
Tom 3.

Note.

makes against it, as the holy *Abbot Ni-lus* noteth very well. There be other good workes, which the diuell is better content to passe withall, and to endure. He will permit sometymes, a *fast*, a *discipline*, and a *hayrecloth*, but a tyme of *Prayer* he cannot endure; but by all possible meanes, he procures to hinder it.

From hence it growes, that when we are in Prayer, we suffer many tymes more temptations, then in any other action of ours. It seemes that then, the whole troupe of thoughts set vpon vs, and sometymes they are so filthy, and so wicked, as if we went not so much thither to pray to God, as to be molested and vexed, with all kinde of temptations by the Diuell. For things which before did neuer present themselues to vs, nor neuer passed by our thoughts, in our whole life, do offer themselues to vs in Prayer; as if they kept themselues of purpose for vs, against that tyme. And since the Diuell knowes, that Prayer is the redresse of all our miseryes, and the beginning, and fountaine of all our spiri-

spirituall good, and an efficacious meanes for the obteyning of all vertue, it puts him to much payne, and he imployeth all the power he hath to hinder it. And so the Saints are wont to call Prayer, *Tormentum Damonum*, & *flagellum Damonum*. The torment, and the scourge of the Diuell.

This very thing ought to be a cause, and motiue to vs, to make vs more to esteeme, and more diligently to frequent the vse of Prayer: and so much the more, because the Diuell, out of a meere enuy which he beares vs, seekes to hinder vs. *S. Thomas* of *Auila* and other graue Authors affirme, that for this very reason, our Holy Mother the *Church* who is gouerned by the *Holy Ghost*, and knoweth well, that the custome of our enemy, is to tempt, and make all the war he can vpon them who are in Prayer; hath ordeyned, that at the beginning of euery one of her Canonicall howers, this verse be said : *Deus in adiutorium meum intende : Domine ad adiuuandum me festina.* Where we desire fauour of our Lord, that he will enable vs to pray as

we

Thomas Abulensis.

Noted.

Psal. 69. 2.

Note. we ought, and defend vs from the ambushes, and temptations of our enimies.

Thirdly, thefe vayne thoughts, and *Diſtractions*, do ſometymes grow vpõ vs in Prayer, without any fault of ours, and only out of our very infirmity and weakeneſſe. For we are ſo fraile, and miſerable, and our nature doth remaine ſo totally diſordered, & decayed by ſinne, and eſpecially our *imigination*, that we can ſcarce ſay a *Pater noſter*, but diuers thoughts wilbe offering at vs, according to the complaint of *S. Bernard*. For this, it wilbe a good remedy, that we take for the ſubiect of our *Prayer*, the conſideration of that thing, which makes vs ſuffer, and ſo to humble our ſelues, by the knowledge and ſenſe of our owne great miſery. For this *Humility*, & this *knowledge of our ſelues*, wilbe a very good *Prayer*: though yet beſides, we will ſpeake of ſome other remedyes, which are giuen by the Maiſters of ſpirituall life, and other holy men.

CHAP.

Chap. XXII.

Of other remedies, for the making vs re-
maine with attention, and reuerence,
in our Prayer.

THE blessed *S. Basil*, asketh how
a man may growe to haue a firme, and attentiue hart in Prayer; and
he answeareth, that the most efficacious meanes for this, is to consider,
that he is in *the presence of God*; & that
God is looking how he prayes. For if
here, a man standing before a Prince,
and speaking with him, do carry himselfe with great respect, & reuerence;
and do apply great attention to what
he doth, and to the manner & fashion
which he holds therein; and should
esteeme it for an act of great ill-man-
ners in himselfe, to turne his back towards the Prince, yea or yet to vse any
impertinent discourse with him: what
shall that man do, who attentiuely
considereth, that he stands in presence
of the Maiesty of God; and that he is
looking on; and that not only vpon
the

Basilius in
regulis
breuiori-
bus 201. *&*
306. *& in*
constitu-
tionibus
ad solita-
rios.

the exterior, but vpon the moſt ſecret, and internall parte of his hart. Who (ſayth he) is that man, that ſhall preſume to diuert his eyes, and his hart, from that which he is doing; and ſhall aduenture to turne his backe to God, and paſſe his thoughts, in that place, towards impertinent things?

That great *Monke Iacob*, as *Theodoret* recounts, doth vſe this following conſideration, to ſhew what a great irreuerence this would be, and it is alſo alledged by *S. Auguſtine*. If I (ſaid he) were the ſeruant of a man, who is alſo of the ſame nature with my ſelfe; and at the tyme when I were to ſerue him, ſhould leaue to bring him his dinner, through the will which I might haue to be talking with ſome fellow-ſeruant of mine; my Maiſter might reprehend, and puniſh me, with iuſt reaſon. And if being before a Iudge, to complayne of ſome body, who had done me wrong, I ſhould leaue him, euen as the word were in my mouth; and ſhould turne my backe towards him, and ſtand talking with others who were there; do you not thinke,

Theodoret. in hiſtoria Sanctorum Patrum c. 21. Auguſt. ſuper Pſa. 85.

                                              that

that he would take me, to be a rude
fellowe, and commaund me to be
caſt out of the *Tribunall*, where he were
giuing ſentence? Now this is that
which they do, who going to treat
with God in *Prayer*, do yet diſtract
themſelues, by thinking of impertinent things. Our *B. Father* preſcribeth
alſo this helpe, which followes, in
one of the *Additions*, or *Aduertiſements*,
which he ſets downe for *Prayer*. Where
he ſayth, that immediatly before we
enter into Prayer, we ſhould, for the
ſpace of a *Pater noſter*, lift vp our ſpirit
to heauen, and conſider that the ſame
God is preſent with vs heere; and that
he is looking vpon vs, and that ſo, we
ſhould begin our Prayer, with great
humility and reuerence. And we are
to procure, that this *Preſence of God*, be
not loſt by vs in the whole tyme of
our *Meditation*, according to that of the
Prophet: *Et meditatio cordis mei, in conſpectu
tuo ſemper.*

    S. Chryſoſtome ſayth: *Make account
that when you go to Prayer, you are entring
into that celeſtiall Court, where the king of
glory is ſeated, in heauen, which is all imbro-*
dered

*Ignatius
lib. exer-
citiorum
ſpiritua-
lium*

*Pſa. 18 15.
Chryſoſt.
ſuper illud
Pſal. 4.
Miſerere
mei, &
exaudi
orationem
meam.*

dered *with stars*, and that King *inuironed
with innumerable angells and Saints, & that
they all stand, beholding vs, according to that
of* S. Paul : *Spectaculum facti sumus mundo
& angelis & hominibus.* S. *Bernard* counselleth how we are to carry our selues
herein. *Veniens ad Ecclesiam, pone manum
tuam super os tuum, & dic: Expectate hic cogitationes, mala intentiones, & affectus cordis, & appetitus carnis: tu autem anima mea,
intra in gaudium Domini Dei tui, vt videas
voluptatem Domini, & visites templum eius.*
Whē thou shalt enter into the Church,
and recolect thy selfe towards Prayer,
lay thy hand vpon thy mouth, & say:
Stay you here at the gate, you disor-
dered thoughts, and appetites; & thou
O my soule, enter into the ioy of thy
Lord, that thou maist see, and do his
holy *will.*

S. *Iohn Climacus*, sayth; *That he who
when he is in* Prayer *considereth in good earnest, that he is standing in the presence of*
God, is a firme & cōstant pillar, which
cannot *be moued.* And he relates, how
that seeing, at a certayne tyme, a *Religious mā*, who was more attentiue then
the rest, in the singing of *Psalmes*, and
that

1.Cor.4.9.

Bernardus.
Climacus
in scala
spirituali
gradu. 4.
§. 18.

that especially, at the beginning of the
Hymns he seemed, by the manner and
countenance which he held, as if he
had beene speaking with another, he
desired him afterward, that he would
tell him, what the matter was. The
monke made him this answere: *At*
the beginning of the diuine Office, I am wont
to recollect my hart, and thoughts, with great
care; and calling them before me, I vse to say,
Venite adoremus, & procidamus, & ploremus
ante Dominū qui fecit nos, quia ipse est Domi- Psa.94.6.
nus Deus noster, nos autē populus eius, & oues
pascua eius. Come let vs adore and pro-
strate our selues, let vs weepe before
our Lord; because he is our Lord, and
our God, and we are his people, and
the sheep of his pasture. All these cō-
siderations are very profitable, and
good, to make vs pray with reuerence,
and attention.

Others giue this remedy; to put our
selues before the *B. Sacramēt*, if we be in
place where we may do it. Or if not, to
be as neere the *B. Sacrament* as we can,
and there to lodge our hart. It is also
good, to haue an eye vpon holy *Ima-*
ges. Others helpe themselues by looking

king vp to heaué. It is alfo very good, to quicken a man, when he is fubiect to *diftractions*, and drynesse, in *Mentall Prayer*, to caft out fome *Iaculatory Prayers*, and to fpeake vocally to God; reprefenting our weakenes to him, and thus demanding remedy thereof, *Domine vim patior, refponde pro me.* O Lord anfwere thou for me, for I fuffer violence. That *Blinde man* of the *Gofpell*, although Chrift our Lord feemed to diffemble the care he had, and did paffe wide of him; and although the people bad him hold his peace; yet be neuer gaue ouer to cry out, but rayfed his voyce, fo much the more; and exclaimed faying, *Iefu filÿ Dauid miferere mei*, I ES VS the Sonne of Dauid, haue mercy on me. *Confirma me Deus in hac hora.* Strengthen O Lord, and confirme this hart of mine, in this hower; to the end that it may be able to thinke of thee, and to be firme, and conftant in my Prayer.

A holy woman gaue this Counfel. If you cánot fpeake to God with your hart, fayle not to fpeake often to him, with your mouth; for that which is
fpo-

Note.

Ifa. 58. 14.

Mark. 10. 47.
Luc. 18. 18.

Iudi. 13. 9.

S. Angela
de Fulgin.
ca. 58. &
26.

fpoken fo frequently, doth eafily giue heat, and feruour to the hart. And this Saint confeffeth of her felfe, that fom-tymes, through failing to vfe *vocall Prayer,* fhe loft that which was *mentall,* through her being fo preft and hin-dred, now and then, by flouth, and fleepe. This alfo is our owne cafe. A man now and then, forbeares to fpeake in his Prayer, out of very floth, and being halfe a fleepe ; whereas if he would fpeake, he might awake, and reuiue himfelfe, for Prayer.

Gerfon fayth, That it is a good re-medy againft *Diftractions,* to haue the *Meditation* well prepared, and the *Points* diftinguifhed *for Prayer.* For ther-by, when one is diftracted, and re-flects vpon it, he hath already his *Point,* which is certayne and determi-ned, to his hand, to which he may re-tire. And if that prooue not with him, he may inftantly paffe to another of thofe *Points,* which he had prepared, & returnes the more eafily, to fpin on the thred of his Prayer. And we finde by experience, when we examine our felues, that many tymes the caufe of

Gerfon.

Note.

N   our

our being *distracted* , and that we go
wandring , vp and downe to diuers
things, is becaufe we haue not our
Points well prouided, and knowne,
vpon which we may make our Prayer, and fo we want a place , to which
we may retire our felues.

Moreouer , not only the aduife,
which now I giue , but that alfo
which followes, is very neceffary, to
the end that we may go well prepa-

Ignatius
l. Exercit.
fpiritua-
lium nota-
bile 1.
hebdoma-
dæ. 4 .

red for Prayer. And fo our B. *Father*
doth recommend it to vs, in very fe-
rious words. *Magnopere iuuabit ,ante in-*
greffum Exercij, tractanda puncta commi-
nifci , & numero certo præfinire. It will
greatly help , fayth he , if before we
go to praier, we recapitulate the points
whereupon we are to meditate , and
do appoint a certaine number of them.
And we read of him , that himfelfe v-
fed this methode ; and that , not onely
in his beginnings , but afterward alfo,

Note.

when he was an old man. And he prepared his *Exercife* ouer night, and wet
to reft , with that care vpon him. I relate this , to the end, that no man may
thinke , that this diligence is onely to

be

be vſed by *Nouices*. Yea and although a man do already know the exerciſe well, as hauing meditated vpon it at other tymes, neuertheleſſe, it wilbe very well done for him, to prepare himſelfe againe. For thoſe words wherupon we *pray*, being vſually of the *holy ſcripture*, and therfore dictated by the *Holy Ghoſt*, the very reading them, with a quiet and repoſed mind, will rayſe a new attention, and deuotion, to meditate, and profit by them, ſo much the more.

Againe, it wilbe of much helpe, if preſently when we awake, we giue no place to other thoughts, but thinke of the *Exerciſe* which we are to make; preparing our ſelnes for Prayer, by ſome conſideration, accommodated to that which we are to *meditate*. *Caſſian, S. Bonauenture*, and *S. Iohn Climacus*, do hold this, for a very important aduiſe. And they ſay, that the order of our Prayer, and conſequently the diſpoſition of the whole day after, doth much depend heerupon. And *S. Iohn Climacus* doth obſerue, that wheras the diuell doth well ſee, that this particu-

Bonauent. in informat. nouitiorum. p. 1. c. 4. Cùm euigilas, ſtatim omnes cogitationes tuas abijce de corde tuo, & offer Deo primitias cogitationum tuarum. Climacus c. 21.

N 2   ler

ler is of much importance ; he is therfore very diligent, and follicitous , in
watching, when we chance to wake;
to the end , that inftantly he may
take vp his lodging with vs; and fo,
gather the firft fruits of the whole day.
And he fayth , that there is amongft
thofe maligne fpirits, one, whome
they call the *Precurfor*, who hath the
office to watch, and fet vpon vs by
night, at the tyme when we firft a-
wake, out of our fleep, yea and a little
before we are fully awake , when a
man is fcarce returned entirely vnto
himfelfe; that fo he may reprefent certaine deformed filthy things to our
mind, or at leaft, things impertinent;
therby taking the poffeffion for the
whole day; for he conceiues, that the
hart wilbe his, who is firft poffeffed
therof.

For this reafon , it will import vs
much,that we be full of caution , in
giuing no place to our enemy, but
that inftantly, when euen we haue
fcarce opened our eyes , the memory
of our Lord,may be already planted in
our harts, before any other thought be
lodged

lodged there. Wherof our B. *Father,*
doth also aduise vs : & he addeth moreouer, that the same guard, is, after a
sort, to be held by vs, ouer our selues,
when we are to make Prayer, at any
other houre, by recollecting our selues a little, to thinke, *Whither go I, and
before whome do I purpose to appeare?* and
by recapitulating briefly the mystery
whereupon you are to *meditate*, like
one who tunes the instrument, before
he playes. And our B. *Father* said, that
generally the making of good Prayer,
and gathering store of Fruite therby,
did in great parte depend vpon the
obseruation of these, and the like ad-
uises, which he calleth *Additions.* And
our selues do very ordinarily find the
truth of this, by experience; and that
when we go well prepared, and take
care to follow these directions, our
Prayer proues very well; and if not,
otherwise.

The holy Ghost sayth, by the *Wise-
man; Ante orationem præpara animam tuam,
& noli esse quasi homo, qui tentat Deum.* Before Prayer prepare your selues for it,
and be not like the man who tem-

*Ignatius
li. exerci-
tiorum
Spiritua-
lium addit.
2. prioris
hebdoma-
dæ. & ad-
dit. 5. se-
cundæ heb-
domadæ.
& in 1.
modo ora-
di.*

Eccl. 18.

pteth

S. Tho. 2.
2.q.97.ar.
3. ad 2.
Bonauent.
in opuscu-
lo cui ti-
tulus est,
Regula
nouitioru
ca. 2.

pteth God. *S. Thomas* & *S. Bonauenture,*
note, vpon thefe words, that to go to
Prayer, without preparation, *is to tempt*
God. *For to tempt God,* fay the *Deuines, is to*
defire any thing without imploying the vfuall,
and neceffary meanes, of obtayning it. As if
one fhould fay, *I will not eate becaufe*
God can, and will fufteyne me, without ea-
ting. This fhould be *a tempting of God,*
and a demaunding of a miracle, without neceffity. As Chrift our Lord faid

Note.

to the diuell, when he tooke him vp,
to a pinnacle of the *Temple,* and per-
fwaded him *that he should cast himfelfe*
downe, and that God would command his
Angells to take and carry him, in the palmes
of their hands; For our Lord anfwered

Matt. 4.7.

thus. *Non tentabis Dominum Deum tuum.*
Thou shalt not tempt thy Lord, and thy God,
I may go downe by a ladder; this o-
ther is a tempting of God, and a demaund of a miracle without neceffity. Since therfore the preparation of
our felues to Prayer, is fo principall, &
fo neceffary a meanes, to the thing it
felfe, that the *Wifeman* fayth, *That to re-*
folue to haue Prayer, without this prepara-
tion is a kind of tempting of God, and a pre-
                              tending,

tendind to haue him ſhewe miracles
with you, our Lord is well pleaſed
that we haue good Prayer, and that
we performe it with much attention,
and reuerence; but yet he deſireth that
we ſhould haue it, by the ordinary
meanes, wherof we haue ſpoken.

Chap. XXIII.

Of a matter of great conſolation, for them
who are moleſted, & diſtracted in Praier.

FOr the comfort of ſuch as are moleſted with this temptation, S. *Ba-*
ſil notes, that in *Prayer*, we onely then
offend God by theſe *diſtractions*, and
thoughts, when a man, with his will,
and after reflection made vpon what
he doth, is *diſtracted*, & caryeth himſelf
with litle reuerence, and reſpect. He
who putteth himſelfe to *Prayer*, and
therein doth purpoſely thinke of his
ſtudy, or of his *office*, or of his *buſineſſe*,
doth well deſerue that God ſhould not
help, but puniſh him. And here that
comes well in, which S. *Chryſoſtome*
ſayth, *Tu non audis orationem tuam*, &

Baſil. in
conſtit.
monaſti-
cis. ca. 2.

Note.

Chryſoſt.
ho. 17. in
varia loca
Matt. 10.

N 4   *Domi-*

Dominum vis audire precem tuam, ? With what reason canst thou expect, that God should heare thee, when thou dost not so much as heare thy selfe ?

But on the other side, when a man doth morally what he can, and yet is *distracted*, through weaknes, & cannot haue so much attetion, as he desires, but doth as it were forsake his hart, & fly abroad, according to that of the Prophet, *Cor meum dereliquit me* ; then our Lord is not offended with him ; but rather is moued to compassion, and mercy, becausehe well knoweth our infirmity, and weakenes. *Quomodo miseretur pater filiorum, misertus est Dominus timentibus se ; quoniam ipse cognouit figmentum nostrum.* As a Father who hath a Sonne, sick of a frenzy, suffereth with him, and is much afflicted, when he heares, that for euery word that he speakes of sense, he talkes idlely afterward ; so our most mercifull, celestial father, doth pitty, and hath compassió of vs, whé he considers that the weaknesse, and infirmity of our nature is so great, as that whé it imports vs most to to be speaking, in our wits, we flye out

Psa.39.13.

Psa. 102. 13.

out into a thousand absurd thoughts.

And so although a man feele no deuotion & finde no iuyce in Prayer, but much drynesse, and combat of imaginations, and thoughts; and although he continue so, all the tyme of his Prayer; yet that very Prayer, leaues not to be very gratefull to our Lord God, and of great value, & merit, in his diuine presence. Nay it vseth many tymes, to be more gratefull, & meritorious, then if a man had passed through it, with much deuotion, and consolation; in regard that he hath endured, and suffered that difficulty, and trouble in that Prayer, for the loue of God. Neyther doth the same **Note:** Prayer, leaue to obteyne grace & fauour, wherewith to serue our Lord better, and to increase more in vertue, and perfection, although he feele it not then. As it happeneth to a sicke man, who feeds vpon some meat of substance; & although he take no delight, nor feele no taft therein, but payne and torment; yet he getteth strength, and growes therby towards a recouery.

By

Note.

By that which is ſaid, it may be
eaſily ſeene, how great an errour, and
how grieuous a temptation it is, for a
man to giue ouer his Prayer, becauſe
he findes it ſubiect to great variety of
thoughts and temptations. Onely it is
needfull, to be well aduertiſed, that v-
pon this occaſion, & vnder colour of
I can no more, tepidity and ſloath doe
not enter in ; and that we be not facill
Tract. 8.
ca. 50.
and remiſſe, to be carryed away with
all windes ; and to ſuffer our thoughts
to go wandering, and our imagination to be where it liſts, as afterward
I ſhall touch more at large ; but that
we performe, all that which is to be
done on our parte ; procuring with
great care, & diligence to haue an eye,
Geneſ. 15.
11.
& to driue away thoſe thoughts, as the
holy *Abraham* did the birds, which
deſcended ouer the *Sacrifice*. But doing (as is ſayd) that which morally
is in our power, there is no cauſe, why
Refert
Bloſius ca.
3. monit.
ſpiritual.
we ſhould trouble our ſelues.

We reade of *S. Brigit*, that when
ſhe was tired in her Prayer with many temptations', our *Bleſſed Lady* appeared to her, and ſaid: Thus the Di-
ueſl

uell being enuious at the good of me, «
procures, as much as he may, to giue «
them difficultyes and impediments, «
when they are in Prayer; but thou O
Daughter, with whatſoeuer tempta- «
tion,and how wicked ſoeuer, thou be «
moleſted in that Exerciſe, & though it «
ſeeme to thee that thou canſt not poſſi- «
bly driue it away; yet procure thou «
neuertheleſſe, to continue aſwell as «
thou maiſt, in that good will of thi- «
ne, and in thoſe holy deſires;and this
ſhalbe a very good, and a very profitable Prayer,and it ſhalbe of great me- «
rit in the ſight of God. We haue already ſpoken, els where, of a very good
meanes for the reſtoring of that which
we may ſeeme to haue loſt, by our *di-*
ſtractions.

CHAP. XXIV.

Of the Temptation of Sleepe*, and from*
whence it comes, and the remedies
therof.

THE temptation of *Sleepe,* which
is another kind of *diſtraction,* may
ſome-

ſometimes proceed from a naturall cauſe, as by want of ſleepe, much wea-rynes, ill weather, exceſſe of age, ex-ceſſe of eating, or of drinking, althogh it ſhould be but of water. Thoſe an-cient holy Fathers of the *Deſert*, did re-late, how God ſhewed to them in ſpirit, that there were certaine *Diuells*, who did ſet themſelues vpon the necks, and heads of *Monkes*, and made them ſleepe. And others who put cer-taine fingers into their mouthes, and made them yawne. At other tymes, this groweth from our ſloath, and ne-gligence, when a man is in Prayer, in ſome ſuch compoſition of his perſon, as may giue occaſion to *Sleepe*. The chiefe remedy for this, is that which was ſaid before, concerning attention; and to remember that we are in the *preſence* of Almighty God. And, as a man who is in the preſence of ſome great Prince, will not preſume to ſleepe; ſo we, who conſider that we ſtand before the maieſty of God, and that he is beholding vs, ought to be much confounded in our ſelues, when we ſleepe in *Prayer.*

Cap. 22.

It

It is also a good remedy to ſtand on foote, without leaning; and to waſh our eyes with cold water; and ſome vſe to carry a wet napkin about them, if they be much oppreſſed with this temptatio. Some help themſelues, by looking vp to heauen; and by making Prayer, where there is much light; or els to pray in preſence of the B. *Sacrament,* in company of others; or to take a diſcipline before Prayer, wherby they may remaine, both awake, & deuout. Others, whilſt they are *Praying,* giue themſelues ſome kinde of little payne, whereby they keepe thcmſelues awake; & when they pray alone, they ſpread their armes, into the forme of a *Croſſe.* It helpeth alſo for this, to ſpeake, and ſay ſome *Vocall Prayers,* wherby a man may be ſtirred vp and much reuiued, as we ſaid before. It is good to ſerue our ſelues of theſe, and ſuch other remedyes, beſeeching our Lord, that he will cure this infirmity of ours.

Ceſarius, in his dialogues, doth recount of a *Religious man* of the *Ciſterſian Order,* (who vſed to ſleepe many tymes

Cap. 22.

Ceſarius li. 4. *dialog. c.* 29.

tymes in *Prayer*,) that there appeared
to him Chriſt our Lord, being crucifyed, with his back turned towards
him; and then he ſaid, *Why art thou ſo
negligent and ſlothfull ? Thou doeſt not deſerue to ſee my face.* Of another he recounteth there, that God did giue him
a more ſharp reproofe, becauſe being
in the *Quire* at *Prayer*, and ſleeping as
he vſed, a *crucifix* came to him from the
Altar, and gaue him ſuch a blow vpon
the cheeke, that he dyed of it the third
day after. All this, giues vs well to vn-
derſtand, how much this negligence
and tepidity dipleaſeth God. The te-
pid, and negligent *Religious man* (as *Caſarius* ſayth) doth prouoke God, as if it
were to vomit; according to that of
the *Apocalyps: Becauſe thou art tepide, I will
caſt thee out of my mouth.*

Of *S. Romualdus* the Abbot (who
was the founder of the order of *Camal-
dula*,) it is related by *Petrus Damianus*
(ſpeaking of the *Prayer* which his *Religious* men did make) that it was, in the
account of that Saint, ſo great a fault
to ſleepe in *Prayer*, that he permitted
not ſuch a one to ſay *Maſſe* that day; for
the

*Caſarius
lib. 4. c.
38.*

*Apoc. c. 3.
16.*

Romual-
dus Ab-
bas.

the little reuerence wherewith he had remained, in the presence of our Lord, whome he was to receiue.

<h2>CHAP. XXV.</h2>

How much it importeth vs to take some extraordinary tyme, for the giuing of our selues to Prayer.

AS the men of this world, besides the ordinary, and daily refection of their bodyes, haue their extraordinary Feasts, and banquets, wherein they exceed their common course; so also is it very fit, that besides our dayly *Prayer,* we should also haue our spirituall feasts, and banquets; where our soules may not eate by so strict measure, as at other tymes; but may be filled by the abundance, and sweetnes of the grace of our Lord. Nature it selfe teacheth this. For we see, that the ground is not content, with the dew which falleth, night by night; but it requires sometymes, that it should rayne a whole weeke, or two, without ceasing; and all is little inough, to

the

the end, that it may remaine so well
imbrued, with water, as that the suc-
ceeding *Winde*, and *Sunne* may not dry
it vp. So also it is fit for our soules,
that, besides the ordinary dew of euery
day, they may haue some set tymes,
wherein they may procure to fill
themselues so well with vertue, and
with the very iuyce of deuotion, as
that the *Sun*, or *Winde* of future businesse, and temptations, or the other ac-
cidents of the world, may not serue
to dry them vp. And so we read of
P. Francis- many *Saints*, and *Prelates* of the *Church*,
cus Arias that leauing their imployments, and
p.2.del a- businesse, they did often recolect the-
proue cha- selues, for some tyme, in retired places;
miento es-
piritual. so to giue themselues the more to
tract.5.de *Prayer*, and diuine *Contemplation.* We
la oration read of the holy *Abbot Arsenius*, that he
cap.7. had for a custome, to take some day in
the weeke, for this purpose, which
was the *Saturday*; at which tyme he
continued from the euening therof, till
the next day morning, in *Prayer.*

This is very important, not only
Note. for the aduancing, and improuing our
selues more in vertue, and perfection,
but

but euen for the not returning back-
ward. For so great is the weakenes &
misery of man, and the inclination
which we haue to ill; that although
sometymes we begin our *spirituall
Exercises* with feruour, yet we instantly
go decaying, by little and little, and
vnsaying that, which we professed
before. Like water, which how high
soeuer it boile, yet by retiring it from
the fire, it doth presently, by little and
little, returne to the naturall coldenes.
So do we returne instantly to our tepidity, and slacknesse; which we seeme
to haue more rooted in vs, and more
connaturall to vs, then water hath to
coldenes. *Sensus enim, & cogitatio humani
cordis, in malum prona sunt, ab adolescentia
sua,* sayth the *Holy Ghost*. *Quoniam ne-
quam est natio eorum, & naturalis malitia
ipsorum* For as we are *nothing*, so we are
still returning to our *nothing*.

    To this may be added, that since
we are so full of imployments, some
of vs in *studies*, others in particuler *mi-
nisteries*, others in *Offices* and *exterior businesse*; we haue so much the more need,
of this particuler kind of *Recollection*.

Gen. 3. 21.

Sap. 12. 10.

Note

    O   For

For although our bufineffe be good,
and holy; yet as the knife is dulled by
being dayly vfed, and, from tyme to
tyme, it is neceffary to giue it a new
edge ; fo we grow dayly dull, and be
forgetting our owne fpirituall profit,
whilft we fet forward, that of others.
Euen the Philofophers could tell vs,
that, *Omne agens, agendo repatitur. Euery*
agent, doth euen by doing , fuffer, and part
with fomewhat of his owne; & euery
man findes this by experience in himfelfe. It doth therfore importe vs very
much, to recolle&t our felues at certayne tymes, and to vntye our mindes
from all other imployments; to redreffe this loffe, and to repaire that,
which is decaying dayly in vs, and to
recouer new forces for the future. Fcr
we are yet more obliged, to helpe our

3 p. tract. felues then our neighbours, and *Charity*
c. 4. l. 8. *well ordered beginnes at home.*

This is alfo to be done, with great
care, fince it importeth fo much, euen
for the very *End* of helping our neigh-
Note. bours. For a moft certayne thing it is,
that from our owne greater fpirituall
profit, doth alfo grow the greater fpirituall

rituall profit of our neighbours. And therfore, that tyme is not loſt to them, which any man takes for himſelfe; but rather they ſhall grow rich, by it. It is like the letting of land lye fallow for this yeare, to the end that it may fructi-fy ſo much the more, the next. Father *Auila* ſaid, that it was like the moul-ding of a ſtone, to the end that it may be made able to *grind*. And ſo a mãs be-ing to much in buſines, is ſo far from being any reaſon, why he ſhould not recolect himſelfe, as that for the ſame very cauſe, and ſo much the more, as a man is imploied, & much imbarked in *miniſteryes*, and *buſineſſes*, in ſo much the more neceſſity he is, of reſorting to this remedy. They who go ſayling far by ſea, haue need to take *Porte* many ty-mes, to refreſh themſelues, and take in neceſſary, & new prouiſions. And ſo they, who go imbarked in *buſineſſe*, & *miniſteries*, and *imployments* with their neighbours, and who are in ſo many dangers, and occaſions of ſinne; haue need many tymes, to make recourſe to to the *Port* of ſolitude and recolection, that ſo they may take in new & neceſ-

ſary

M. Auila.

fary prouifions ; and dreffe vp, & prouide themfelues, of what is fit.

In the holy Gofpell, we haue an
excellent example of this. The *Euan-
gelift S. Marke*, recounteth how the A-
poftles went full of bufineffe, in the
Imployments which they had, concerning their neighbours ; in fuch fort
as that they had fcarce tyme to eate, fo
great was the nûber of people which
was offered to them. They went to
giue account, to Chrift our Lord, of
that which paffed heerin ; and he faid
to them, *Come a part into the defert, and
repofe awhile?* Recollect your felues a
while, in the folitude of the *defert*. If
then the Apoftles had need of repofe,
and recolection, and that our *B. Sauiour*
himfelfe did counfell it to them, how
much more need therof haue we ?

They who treat of *Prayer*, fay very
well, that *Prayer is that to the foule, which
repofe and fleepe is to the body*. And fo, the
holy fcripture calleth it *fleepe: Ego dormio,
& cor meum vigilat. Adturo vos filiæ Ierufalem, ne fufcitetis, neque euigilare faciatis dilectam, donec ipfa velit.* And declaring
this more at large, they fay, of the body,

Cant.5. 2.

Cant.8. 4.

dy, that when it reposeth by corporall
sleepe, it resteth and recouereth new
force and strength, and so the soule, re-
posing in the sleepe of *Prayer*, recouereth also fresh breath, and life, wherewith to labour, in the seruice of Al- Note.
mighty God. And more then this. As
a man who feedeth vpon good meat,
yet if he want repose, and necessary
sleepe, will prooue but weake & sicke,
yea and also be in danger, to loose his
wits; so also he, who shall go greatly
imployed in exterior businesses (how
holy & good soeuer they may be) yet
if he want the necessary repose, & rest
of *Prayer*, he will prooue but weake &
decaied in spirit, and will runne ha-
zard to loose himselfe. And therfore
doth the *Spouse* require, *That they awake*
not his beloued, till she will, herselfe. When
they wake a man out of sleepe, by any
noise which they make, it is a thinge
displeasing to him; but when he wa-
keth of himselfe, because nature is satisfyed, and for that he hath reposed
inough. (in regard that the fumes
which mounted vp to the braine, are
now disgested,) there is no offence
ther-

therein. Iuft fo is it with the foule. Our
Lord requireth, that no man, nor no
thing trouble it, nor hinder the *Prayer*
which fhe is in; but when that reft is
taken which is neceffary, fhe may then
awake herfelfe, and returne to the imployments of the works of *Charity*, and
fo they wilbe well performed.

Although it be of great importance
for all men, and vpon all iuft occafions, to recollect themfelues in *fpiritual Exercifes*, and to giue themfelues
more to *Prayer*, and fo much the more
as we fhall do it, fo much the better it
wilbe; yet particulerly in fome occafions and coniunction of reafons, this
is neceffary. As namely, when a man
fees, that he goes declyning in the *fpirituall Exercifes* of *Prayer*, of *Examen*, of
fpirituall reading, and that now, he ga-
thereth not the fruite, and profit by
it, which were fit: When he feeth that
he growes negligent, and carelefle in
the obferuance of his *Rules*, and that
now, he makes no more accounte of
fmall matters: When he feemes to himfelfe, that he is not fpirituall, and in-
trouerted, but that he is very exterior,
and

Note.

and much carried away, by the occasions, and businesses which he treates:
When he also obserueth, that he doth
not ouercome, and mortify himselfe
out right, in some one thing; it is very
good for him to recollect himselfe,
some dayes, in these *Exercises*, that so he
may finish the resolution, to conquer
himselfe. For it may be, that in one of
these *Recollections*, he may obteyne
more grace of our Lord, and more
strength wherewith to mortify, and
ouercome himselfe, then by the labour
of many dayes.

Many tymes it happeneth, that a
man goes lymping; he riseth, and he
falleth, and in some one of these *Exercises*, he remaineth vnbeguiled of the
vanity of the world, and fully possessed of *Truth*, and resolute to do all
that is fit. He changeth his style, & he
takes a new manner of life vpon him.
For in fine, the being so long alone,
treating with God, and with himselfe,
is a great dispositió, to make our Lord
speake to his hart, and to induce his
Maiesty to do many fauours. *Sedebit so-*
litarius, & tacebit, quia leuauit se super se. *Tren.3.28*

O 4

A man doth raise himselfe, aboue himselfe, & makes himselfe, quite another man. And so we haue seene very extraordinary changes, wrought in men by this meanes. *Et non est abbreuiata manus Domini.*

Isa. 59. 1.

We must neuer disconfide in God, but be euer doing that, which is of our part. How do you know, what God will worke in your soule, by meanes of this disposition? It may be, that our Lord hath resolued to grant the spirituall profit, and perfection of your soule, in one of these *Exercises*.

Againe, after the hauing ended some very long iourney, or some busines, or imployment of extraordinary distraction ; this kind of *Recollection*, seemeth to be as important, as good & dainty treaty, is to a body, after a long disease, to the end that a man may recouer himselfe, & repaire the strength which he hath lost. And for the same reason, it is also very good, for a man to prepare himselfe beforehand, by these *Exercises*, when he findes that he is growing into some such kind of businesse; to the end that he may do things with more vertue, and lesse spirituall

losse

loſſe of his owne. The *Preſeruatiue*, is a better kinde of *Phiſicke*, then the *Remedy*, which comes after the *diſeaſe*. And therefore *our B. Father*, did recommend to all ſuperiors, that before they began to enter vpon their office, they ſhould make the *Exerciſes*, for ſome days. The ſame is alſo good, when one is to go into ſome long *Miſsion* Wherof Chriſt our Lord gaue vs an example. For before he began to preach, he retired himſelfe *fourty days, into Deſert*. Alſo in a tyme of tribulations, and afflictions, whether they be generall of the whole *Church*, or of his owne *Order*, or of his owne perſon, the occaſion is very good, for this. For to add more *Prayer*, and more *pennance*, and mortification, hath euer beene a meanes, much frequented in the *Church*, for appeaſing the wrath of God, and obteyning mercy from him.

Matt.4.1?

All theſe are very good occaſions to make a man recolect himſelfe in theſe *Exerciſes*. But indeed we haue no need, to ſtand ſeeking of occaſions. Our owne neceſſity, and intereſt, muſt ſollicite vs to deſire, and procure this benefit

nefit very often. At least, no yeare
ought to passe, without our meeting
with these *spirituall Vacations*. And
when we do it, it must be very much
in earnest, and with the whole hart.
For a thing of so great substance, as
this, must in no case be performed
with ceremony, nor for complement,
or because it is handsome.

Our Lord hath imparted this meanes to the *Society*, in a very particuler
manner, not only for our owne profit, but for the help, and profit of our
neighbour. And therfore, in the *Breues*
of our *Institute*, this is placed for one of
the *Principall meanes*, which the *Society*
hath, for the helping of their neighbours. And this also, is another very
particuler reason, for which *our B. Fa-*
ther will, that we haue much vse of
these *Exercises*. And he placeth it in his
Constitutions, and in the *Rules* of *Priestes*:
Vt in hoc armorum spiritualium genere tra-
ctando, quod Dei gratiâ ad ipsius obsequium
tantopere conferre cernitur, dexteritatem ha-
bere possit. To the end that they may
be very dextrous in the managing of
this kind of Armes, which are so profitable

4. p. Const.
c. 8. 5. reg.
7. Sacerdo.

table for the gayning of others. By this
meanes, our Lord did gayne our *B. Father Ignatius.* By this meanes he gained
his *Companions.* By this meanes, so many others haue beene gayned since, aswell within the *Society,* as without it;
and both in the one, and in the other
sort of men, we haue seene, that our
Lord concurreth, with admirable effects. In fine we are to haue great cō-
fidence, that by this meanes, which
hath beene imparted to vs, in so particuler manner by our Lord, he will
helpe vs much, and do vs many fauours.

To that which is already said, I
will add another thinge, which is very important, and which ought to as-
siste and encourage vs much herein,
which is the singuler fauour & grace,
which the *Sanctity* of *Paul the fifth,* hath
granted in this particuler, to all *Religious men,* in that *Bull,* or *Constitution,*
which he dispatched forth, vpon the
three and twentith of *May,* in the yeare
of our Lord, one thousād six hundreth
and six, which was the first of his *Pon-
tificate;* declaring the *Indulgences,* which
Reli-

Religious men should enioy therby. He there granteth a *Plenary Indulgence*, and remission from all sinne, to all *Religious* persons, of what *Order* soeuer they were, who for the space of ten continued dayes, should make the *spirituall Exercises*; and that, as often as they should make them, they were to obteyne the same *Indulgence*. Wherby it may wel be seene, what estimation his *Holynes* made of this matter, and therby, how much our selues ought to esteeme it. *Ijs verò qui de suorum superiorum licentia, à negotys, per decem dies, alieni in cella commorabuntur, aut ab aliorum conuersatione sepxrati; in piorum librorum, & aliarum rerum spiritualium, animos ad deuotionem, & spiritum inducentium, lectionibus operam suam dederint; addendo sæpe considerationes, & meditationes mysteriorum fidei Catholicæ, diuinorum beneficiorum, quatuor nouissimorum, Passionis Domini nostri Iesu Christi, & aliorum exercitiorum, orationum iaculatoriarum, aut vocalium, saltem per duas horas in diem, & noctem, orationibus mentalibus sese exercendo, faciendo eodem tempore confessionem generalem, aut annualem, vel ordinariam, sanctissimam Eucharistiæ*

stia Sacramentum sumpserint, aut missam ce-
lebrauerint. Quoties, pro quolibet prædictorum
Exercitiorum, plenariam similiter omnium
peccatorum suorum indulgentiam & remis-
sionem, misericorditer in Domino concedi-
mus. And also to all them, who with
the leaue of their Superiours, (hauing
laid businesse a side, and being recollected in their Cell, or separated otherwise, from treating and conuersing
with the rest) shall exercise themselues
for the space of ten days, in the reading
of pious bookes, and vsing other spirituall exercises, which raise the hart to
spirit & deuotiō; accompanying these
things many tymes with the considerations and meditations of the mysteryes of the Catholike Fayth, and of
the benefits of God, and of the *Quatuor*
nouissima, and of the passion of Iesus-
Christ our Lord, and other Exercises
of iaculatory and vocall Prayers; and
making also mentall Prayer, at the
least for two houres of the day; and
making, also within the said tyme,
eyther their Generall, or Annuall, or
Ordinary Confession, and receiuing
the most B. Sacrament of the Eucha-
rist,

rift, or saying Masse; whensoeuer they
shall do the aforesaide Exercises, for
euery tyme, that they so shall do them,
we do mercifully in our Lord, grant a
Plenary Indulgence, and remission of
all their sinnes.

Chap. XXVI.

Of the Fruite *which we are to gather when
we recollect our selues, to make the
spirituall* Exercises.

WE are principally to cast our
eyes, vpon three things,
which we are to procure by these
Exercises. The first is, that we must repaire, and renew our selues, in the ordinary dayly actions which we performe, and that we perfect our selues
in them. *For all our spirituall profit and
perfection, doth consist in doing our ordinary
actions well,* as we said els where. Let
no man thinke, that the performing of
these *Exercises,* is nothing els, but to cō-
tinue recolected there, for a weeke or
two, enioying much tyme of *Prayer.* It
is not so ; but to the end, that he may
depart

Tract. 2.
cap. 18. 2.

Note.

depart frō thence, with ability to make better *Prayer* , and to keep those *Additions* , and *documents* , which are giuen to that purpose , and to make his *Examen* well, and to say, & heare *Masse*, and the *diuine office* , and to read *spirituall bookes* with profit. For this, it is , that a man disimployes himselfe from other businesse, during this tyme, to actuate and exercise his mind in doing those things wel; that so he may go forth, al renued, & accustomed to performe them still, after the same manner .

And so our B. *Father* sayth, that during all the tyme, that the *Exercises* continue (which when they are made completely, are to last for the space of a moneth, there must be a particuler *Examen*, carried vpon the obseruation of the *Additions*; and whether the same *spirituall Exercises* be made with diligence , and exactnes , or no; setting downe the errours which he may haue committed , concerning eyther the one, or the other; to the end that a man may be habituated, and accustomed to do these things from that tyme forward, truly well. This he repeateth many

Ignatius l. Exercit. spiritual- in addit. 5. hebdomad. notabile 4. & in heb- doma 5. & hebd. 3. no- tabile 4. post 2. contempl.

many tymes, as one who well knew, the much good that growes therby. And not only in the *spirituall Exercises* themselues, which is the principall, & which must giue force, and spirit to all the rest; but for all his other exteriour ministeryes, and imployments, a man is to goe, a very good proficient, out of the *Exercises*, fetching breath from thēce, wherewith to do his duty, and to keepe his *Rules*, better then before. So that the Fruite of his *Exercises*, is not to be gathered, for that tyme alone, but principally for the future. And so as that when any man comes forth of the *Exercises*, another man may see, the profit which he hath made, by the actions which he performeth.

The second thing which we are to procure, to draw out of these *Exercises*, is, to ouercome and mortifie our selues, in any vntowardnes, or imperfection, to which he may haue beene subiect. Let euery man cast his eyes vpon those things, in which he vseth to fayle most frequently; or to be a cause to make others fayle, or be scandalized by the disedification which he giueth them.

them. And let him procure to go out
of the *Exercises* very well, and for that
they were principally ordeyned, & it
is theyr *End.* And so, the *Title* which
our *B. Father* giues, to the *Exercises*, is
this in vulgar : *Spirituall Meditations, to
make a man able to ouercome himselfe; & to
direct his desires, and deeds, to the greater seruice of our Lord God.* In such sort, that a
man must procure, to go out of the
Exercises, conuerted, and changed in-
to another man. *Et mutaberis in alium* 1. *Reg.* 10.
virum, as *Samuel* said to *Saul*. *Et in virum* 6.
perfectum: Into a perfect man (as S. Paul
sayth,) that a man may see, by the ef- *Ephe.* 4. 13.
fects, and by the actions, that such a
one, hath made the *Exercises.* That if
before, he loued to be talking, and to
loose his tyme; men may see that now,
he is a louer of silence, & recolection.
If before, he loued to be kindly, and
commodiously vsed; it may be seene,
that now, he is a louer of mortification, and pennance. If before, he were
a man, who vsed to mortify others by
his tongue ; that from that tyme forward, he speakes no more, any such
thinges, as those. If before, he were ne-

P   gligent,

gligent, and carelesse, in the obseruation of his *Rules*, and made noe great
reckoning of small errours; that from
thence forth, he be very obedient, and
very punctuall, and that he maketh
much account, euen of the least omis-
sions ; and that, by the grace of our
Lord, he committeth no fault at all,
of set purpose. For if a man be still to
continue with the same vntoward-
nesse, and errours, and that he will
needs come out of the *Exercises*, as he
went in, for what purpose do they
serue?

Ambr. l. 2.
de pœnit.
c. 10.

S. *Ambrose* tels a certaine thing, of a
Younge man of his tyme, which since
he relates, we may do so too. He had
beene a loste man, and had taken the
broade way, which had offered it
selfe to him. The tyme came, that he
changed his purpose, and retorning afterward to his Citty, he encountred
with his old *Camerado's*, but he went
wide of them. And they maruelling
thereat, and thinking, that he had not

Sal. 2. 20.

knowne them, came to him, and said:
We are they &c. and he answered, *But I*
am not he. For he was changed, and
grown

growne another man. After this manner, are we to be conuerted, and changed, that so we may say with the Apostle; *Viuo ego, iam non ego, viuit verò in me Christus.* I liue, yet now not I ; no longer now liueth he, who liued anciently in the Law, he who persecuted the Church, but Christ is he, who liueth in me. And this sayth *S. Ambrose*; which is also the same which was said by *Christ* our Lord, *Si quis vult venire post me abneget seipsum*; That man (sayth he) denies himselfe, who is changed into another man, and procures already not to be that, which he was wont to be. It is related of our *Father Francis de Borgia*, in his life, that after he had conducted the body of the *Empreße* to *Granada* (where our Lord gaue him great light, and vnbeguiled him concerning the vanity of the world, by that spectacle of death, which was present to him) and returning to the Court, he said that it seemed to him, as if he had found it changed, from what it was. But the truth is, that it was himselfe who was all varied, and changed, by the knowledge, and lighte, which

Hier. super hæc verba.

Ambrose

Math. 16. 24. Lucæ 9. 23.

Lib. 1.c.8. vitæ P. de Borgia.

Note.

P 2 God

God had giuen him. And in this manner, are we to come out of the *Exerci-*
ses, with such new light, and so vnbeguiled, as our Lord is wont to make
men, in the *Exercises*.

Note.

The third thing, vpon which we
are to looke, that we may drawe it out
of the *Exercises*, which indeed doth
follow, vpon that which is already
sayd, is the obteyning of some vertue,
or something belonging to perfection;
and particulerly of that, wherof we
haue greatest need; for they be ordeyned for this, *To roote out Vice, and to plant*
Vertue. Two things sayth the *Saint*, do
help a man much towards God. The
one, to diuert a mans selfe, with great
courage, from that to which his nature
vicioufly inclynes him, which is that
we spake of before. The other, to labour with feruour, for that vertue,
which is most wanting to vs. And so
the *Directory* of the *Exercises*, (speaking
of the way, which we are to hold,
when we recollect our selues to them)
doth aduertise, that all the tyme is not
to be imployed, vpon the *Meditations*,
of the *first weeke*. For them (sayth he)
two

Thomas
de Kempis

Directoriũ
Exercitio.
§. 3.

two or three days will fuffice , to the
end that there may be alfo tyme, to go
to other *Meditations*, from whence we
may drawe more perfection. And a-
mongft others thinges which he placeth there for this purpofe, one is, that
we muft take now and then , fome of
thofe principall *Rules* , in which we
may conceiue, that all the perfection
which we can defire, doth confift. As
that (for example,) which fayth, *That as* Reg. 11. fū:
worldly men loue and feeke honours, fame, & mar ij con,
eftimation of renowne in the world; fo we muft ftit.
loue , and intenfely defire , the very contrary.
Take to hart, in fome one *Exercife* , to
obteyne this perfection, and to arriue
to this *degree of humility,* that you may
be as glad of affronts , difgraces, iniu-
ryes, and falfe teftimonies, as worldly
men are glad of honor, & eftimation ;
and therby you fhall growe to be
Lord ouer many impertinences, and
debates, which vfe to prefent thefelues
to you , vpon the pointe of being valued, & efteemed; more then one , for
his *learning;* and then another , for his
office ; and then another, in the *Minifte-*
ryes of bufineße which he treats ; which
P 3   things

things are wont to inquiet vs, and to
hinder our spirituall profit, very
much.

Take to hart, at some other time,
that rule which sayth: *Let all men, in all
things, procure to serue, and please the diuine
goodnesse, for that goodnes sake it selfe, & for
the loue of it, and for those singuler benefits,
wherewith he preuenteth vs; more then either
for the feare of punishment, or the hope of reward.* Procure you to arriue to this *Pu-
rity of intention*, that you seeke not your
owne interest at all, neither in much,
nor little, neither in the temporall nor
eternall; but in all things, desire truly,
the will, and glory of God, and let this
be your contentment, hauing forgotten your selues, and all your owne interest, and commodity. Take to hart,
another tyme, to obteyne, *A most perfect Conformity, to the will of God,* taking
all things which shall present themselues, eyther great or small, in whatsoeuer manner, or by whatsoeuer way
they come; as being deliuered, by the
hand of God himselfe. Vpon these
poynts of perfection, and other things
like these, we are to cast our eyes, whē
                                    we

we enter into the *Exercises*, and not to
giue ouer, till we obteyne them.

Chap. XXVII.

*Of some directions, which will helpe vs yet
more, to profit by these* Exercises.

TO the end that we may profit
more by these *spirituall Exercises,* &
fetch that Fruite from them, which
hath beene saide, it is to be aduertised,
first (according to what we sayd before) that as when one is going to
Prayer, he is not only to haue those
Points prouided, vpon which he will
Meditate; but also the *Fruite,* which he
is to drawe from thence; so also he,
who is to make the *Exercises,* must, in
particuler, haue that thing ready prouided in his minde, which he meanes
to obteyne by their meanes: & it may
be done after this manner.

   Before he retires himselfe to them,
he is to consider, and treate thus with
himselfe, at much leasure, & attention,
*Which is the greatest spirituall necessity, that
I haue? What is that, to which my vicious in-*
clina-

Cap. 14.

Note:

clination, or my passions, or my ill custome,
doth inclyne me most ? *What is that, which
maketh the stiffest war against my soule ?
What is there in me , wherby my brethren
may be offended, and disedified?* And this is
that which I am to carry before mine
eyes, to the end that I may obteyne it
by my *Exercises,* and may resolue effe-
ctually to amend my selfe. This is a very good preparation, for entring into
the *Exercises* .

Note.   And it is also to be aduertised, that
when a man recollects himselfe, to
make the *Exercises,* he must not propound to himselfe, the obteyning of
very high Prayer; nor to thinke, by that
retiring, and shutting vp himselfe, that
he must presently haue much quietnes, & attention, and familiarity with
almighty God; for it may well happen, that he shall be subiect to more *distractions,* vnquietnes, and temptations,
then when he was in the dispatch of
his *businesse,* and performing his *office*
abroad . But he is to fix his minde, v-
pon fetching that which I haue said ,
out of his *Exercises,* and to resolue himselfe vpon that, in great earnest. And
it

if he obteyne this, he shall haue made
the *Exercifes* very well, though he had
not the deuotion, which he defired.
Whereas if he obteyne not this, although, from the very firft hower he
haue beene euer diffoluing himfelfe in
tears, and deuotion, he shall not haue
made the Exercifes well; for in fine,
that was not the end therof,

That other aduertifement will alfo
help vs much, which our *B. Father*
gaue, and which he will euer haue vs
obferue in *Prayer.* That afterward,
when a man hath ended his hower of *Ignatius*
Prayer, he shall, for a quarter of an *l. Exercit.*
hower, or therabouts, eyther fitting or *fpirituals-*
ftanding, make his *Examen*, of the fame *in addit. 1.*
Prayer. And he shall take account of *hebdomad;*
himfelfe, how it hath prooued with *addit. 5.*
him. If ill, he shall confider the caufe *Note,*
from whence that may haue procee-
ded. He shall confider, if he prepared
his *Exercife* well; if he gaue place to any
impertinēt thoughts; if he fuffred himfelfe to be ouercome with fleepe; if he
deteyned himfelfe too much in the
fpeculation of his *Vnderſtanding.* If his
hart were remiffe, and fainte; and if
he

he did not procure, to exercise the affects of his *Will*. If he had not an intention, as pure as he ought to haue had it; but that he sought his owne comfort, more then the accompliſhment of the diuine will. If he finde himſelfe to haue failed, in any of theſe things, he ſhall repent himſelfe therof, and purpoſe amendment, for the tyme to come. And if it haue prooued well, with him, he ſhall giue thanks to our Lord God, procuring to carry himſelfe after the ſame manner, at his other tymes of *Prayer*.

This document, is of much importance: Firſt, becauſe by this *Examen*, & *Reflection*, which is made, how the *Prayer* hath proued, experience is taken to auoide the faults, and to proſecute that, which was well done; wherby a man obteynes a certaine ſpirituall diſcretion and magiſtery, which groweth from experimentall knowledge. For this reaſon, did our B. *Father*, eſteeme greatly of this *Examen*, and *Reflection*, for the making of ſuch, as might be *Maiſters*, not only in this, but alſo in other imployments, and miniſteries of ours.

ours. And so , in the fourth part of his
Conſtitutions , he ſayth : That it will
greatly helpe a *Ghoſtely Father* , towards the doing of his duty well, to
make *reflection* , and to conſider if he
haue made any fault , in the hearing
of *Confeſsions* . Eſpecially (ſayth he)
let him do it, in his beginnings , ſo to
helpe himſelfe another tyme ; and to
drawe amendemét out of his errours.
For this reaſon therfore, the *Examen of
Prayer*, is to be made. And this is the
firſt thing which we are do therein.
And *Prayer* is of ſo great eſtimation,
and it importeth vs ſo much that we
be accuſtomed to make it well, and to
go ſhredding off the faults which we
make therein; that our *B. Father*, did not
content himſelfe with the *Examen* of
Conſcience, which we vſe to make euery day at *noone*, & at *night*; but inſtantly alſo, aſſoone as we haue ended our
Prayer, his expreſſe pleaſure is, that we
ſhold make a particuler *Examen* therof.

The ſecond thing , (and that a
very principall one) is , that a man is
to conſider the *Fruite*, which he hath
gathered by that *Prayer*, and to returne

4.p. Conſt.
c. 8. litera
D.

Note.

to

to actuate agayne vpon it, (as when
one repeats his lesson) and drawes out
the *Conclusions*, and *Truthes*, which haue
occurred; and makes as it were, an *epi-
logue* of them. And this *Examen*, is to be
held, for a thing of so great importance, that if a man want tyme to make it
after the *Prayer* is ended, he is to make
it in the very *Prayer*, it selfe, in the en-
ding therof.

We may add in this place, another
pointe which will also be of good
vse. That a man set downe, that which
he hath wrought out of his *Prayer* ;
writing the *desires* which he hath had,
and the *Purposes* which he hath made;
but this, must not be done at large, but
in a briefe manner. And so also, let him
set downe, such *Truthes*, and *Illustrations*,
or *Vnbeguilings* of the vanity of this
world, as our Lord is wont to giue
in *Prayer*. Sometymes cócerning some
Vertue, and at other tymes, concerning
the *Mysteryes* themselues, which are in
question. And so we read, that our *First*
Fathers vsed to do, our *B. Father Ignatius*, and Father *Peter Faber* ; and we
haue in our hands, some of those
                                            things

Lib. 9. c. 13
vitæ P.
Fabrij.

things which they wrote hereupon. And *Father Francis Xauerius*, did also aduise the same, as we read in his *life*. And in the *Directory* of the *Exercises*, we haue also the same aduise.

Xauer. c. 2. & 4. Director. Exercitorū spiritual.

And our *Father Generall*, *Claudius Aquauiua*, in the booke of *Industryes*, which he wrote, doth recommend it vnto vs, when he speakes of *Prayer*. For besides, that herby, we perfect our *Purposes*, and *desires* more, and that they growe to be more rooted in our harts; we finde by experience, that a man also profits much in other respects, by reading these things afterward. Because they, hauing been a mans owne, and for that he hath felt them as such; they moue him afterward, more then other things; and he easily actuates vpon them, agayne. And when he findeth afterward, that he arriueth not to the *spirit*, of that he was before; he is confounded, to see, that he is no more the man he was; and that, insteed of aduancing, he is retired. Wherby he will eyther animate himselfe to put on a pace; or els he will supply, by his confusion, that which he shall want of

Claudius Aquauiua in industriis ad curandos animæ morbos c, 3a

perfe~

perfection. So that this, vseth euer to
be of much profit; though especially it
be so, in tyme of the *Exercises* .

3i p. tract.
7. Lastly I say, that if at all tymes, it be
good to giue account of a mans conscience, and of his *Prayer*, to some spirituall man; in this, it wilbe much more
fit. And some, because they will not
humble themselues so far, do not gather, out of the *Exercises*, so much
Fruite, as they might.

Chap. XXVIII.

Of the Reading *of spirituall Bookes ; and
how important it is ; and of some meanes
which may help vs to do it profitably, and
well.*

R EADING, is the Sister, and a
great Helper to *Prayer*. And so the
1. Tim. 4.
13. *Apostle S. Paul*, doth counsell his disci-
ple *Timothy*, *That he should attend to Reading. Attende lectioni.* This *spirituall Reading* is of so great importance, for a
Athana-
sius. man that preteds to serue God, that *S.
Athanasius*, in an exhortation, which he
maketh *to Religious men*, sayth thus: *Sine
legendi*

legendi studio, neminem ad Deum intentum videas. Thou shalt see no body, who indeed pretéds to profit in spirit, who is not also giuen to Reading of spirituall books; & he who leaues it, will quickly shew it , by the state which you shall finde him in. *S. Hierome*, in an epistle to *Eustochium*, recommending much to her, that she giue herselfe greatly to this *sacred Lection,* sayth thus: *Tenenti codicem somnus obrepat, & cadentem faciem pagina sancta suscipiat.* Read , till sleepe take thee; and when, being ouercome by sleepe, thy head is dropping downeward, let those holy leaues receiue it. All the Saints do greatly recommend this *spirituall lection.* And experience telleth vs, how profitable it is; since we see the storyes full of great conuersions, which our Lord hath wrought, by this meanes. *Hierome.*

This *Reading*, is a meanes so principall, & so important, for our spirituall good; that the founders of *Religious orders*, being rooted in the doctrine of the *Apostle*, and in the auctority, and experience of the *Saints*, haue ordeyned, *That their Religious, should euery day , re-*

Vmbertus in Prolog. *Vmbertus* sort to spirituall *Reading.* *Vmbertus* sayth of holy *S. Bennet,* that he ordeyned a set tyme, for this *Reading,* euery day, And he ordeyned with all, that during that tyme, two of the most ancient *Monkes,* should go about the *Monastery,* to visite, and to see, if any did eyther forbeare it themselues, or hinder others. Wherby it may appeare, how much accounte they made therof. And, by the way, we may perceiue, that these *Visites,* which now are daily vsed in *Religion,* at the tyme of spirituall *Exercises,* are grounded in the doctrine, & experience of the ancient *Saints.* For the first, and second tyme, that any failed herein, the *Saint* ordeyned, that he should be reprooued, after a milde fashion; but if he mended not with that, that then they should correct, & giue him such a pennance, as wherby the rest might be kept in feare. In the *Society* we haue *a Rule,* which concernes this *spirituall Reading,* and it speaketh thus: *Let all men, twice in the day, giue that tyme, which is ordeyned, to the Examen of Conscience, and Prayer, and Lection, with all diligence, in our Lord.* And the *Superior*

Regula 1. commun.

perior or Prefect of spirituall matters, hath care that euery one , may depute some tyme, to this purpose, euery day. And generally, this is a helpe for all those who pretend to obtayne vertue, and perfection ; And therfore to the end that they may exercise it with the more *Fruite*, we will here say something, which may conduce therunto.

S. *Ambrose*, exhorting vs , to giue all the tyme we can to *Prayer*, & *spirituall Reading*, sayth : *Cur non illa tempora quibus ab Ecclesia vacas , lectioni impendas? Cur non Christum alloquaris? Christum audias ? Illum alloquimur cùm oramus : illum audimus cùm diuina legimus oracula.* Wherefore doest thou not imploy that tyme , which is free from the Quire, vpon Reading , and Prayer? Why doest thou not goe to visit Christ our Lord ? and both speake to him, and heare him ? For when we pray, he sayth, that we speake to God ; and and when we reade, he speakes to vs. Let this be therfore , the first meanes to profit by *spirituall Reading*, that we make account, *that God is speaking to vs*, & that he speakes euery thing , which
heere

Ambro.li. 1. officior. cap. 20.

Q

heere we *Reade.*

August.
Epist. 143.
ad Deme-
triad. Vir-
ginem.

S. *Augustine* doth also speake of this helpe. *Ita Scripturas sanctas lege, vt sem-per memineris, Dei illa verba esse, qui legem suam non solùm sciri, sed etiam impleri iubet.* Whē thou readest, thou art to make account, that God is saying to thee, that which thou readest, not only that thou mayst know it, but also that thou mayst performe, and put it in practise.

Note.

He addeth another consideration, which is both very good, and very pious. *Diuina scripturæ, quasi literæ de Pa-tria nostra sunt.* Dost thou know, (sayth he) how we are to read the Holy Scriptures ? *As a man would read some letters, which are come to him out of his Coun-try, himselfe being then abroade ; to see what newes there is of Heauen, what they tell vs of that Country of ours ; where our Fathers, and Brothers, and Friendes, and Acquaintance are ; and where we would so faine be, and we long, and sigh to be going thither.*

August.
ser. 36. *ad*
Fra. in
eremo.

Greg. li. 2.
mor. c. 1.

S. *Gregory,* treating of this pointe, sayth that the *holy Scripture* (& the same we may vnderstand of any other *spiri-tuall Reading*) is like the placing of a glasse before the eyes of our soule, to the end that we
may

may see, our inwarde man. For there we
come to know, and playnely see, the
good and bad, that is in vs; and how **Note.**
much we profit; and how far we are
from perfection. And sometymes, there
are related to vs, the admirable deeds
of *Saints*, which may animate vs to
their imitation; and to the end that by
seeing their great victoryes, & triumphs,
we may not be dismaid, at our owne
temptations, and troubles. At other
tymes, there is relation made, not only
of their vertues, but of their fauls, to the
end that by the one, we may knowe
what we are to imitate; and by the
other, what we are to feare. And so
sometymes, there is set before vs, a *Iob*,
who rose vp like foame, by meanes of
temptations; at other tymes, a *Dauid*,
who was drawne downe therby; to
the end that the former may animate
vs, and giue vs confidence in tribula-
tion; and the later, may make vs humble, and timerous, in the middest of
prosperityes and confolations; & may
make vs neuer truft, or be fecure of our
felues, but euer to go on with great
caution, and care. And fo fayth *S. Augu-*
ftine,

Q 2

stine, Optimè vteris lectione diuina, si tibi eam adhibeas, speculi vice, vt ibi velut ad imaginem suam, anima respiciat; & vel sada quaq, corrigat , vel pulchra plus ornet . Then you make good vse of the Reading, *of holy Scriptures* when you take it as a glasse, wherein to view your soule, procuring to correct, and remoue, that deformity and ill, which is reprehended there, and to adorne, and beautify it yet more, by the examples and vertues, which there you finde.

But descending more in particuler, to the way which we are to hold herein, it is to be noted; That to the end that our *Reading,* may be profitable, it must not be hasty, and cursory, as when a man would *read a Story;* but it must be attentiue, and quiet. For as the suddaine and tempestuous rayne, doth not bath, and fertilize the earth; but that is done, by the sweet, & quiet showere; so, to the end that our *reading* may enter, and be steeped more throughly, in the hart, it wilbe fit that it be done with pawse, and ponderation.

And it is good, when we meete with some deuout passage, to deteyne

our

our selues more therein, and to make a
kinde of *Station* vpon it; reflecting v-
pon that which we shall haue *read*;and
procuring to mooue, and effect our
will therby, as we vse to do in *Medita-*
tion. Although in *Meditation*, this must
be done more at large, deteyning our
selues more vpon those thoughts, and
ruminating, and digesting them more.
But yet, the same must be done, to some
proportion, in this *spirituall Reading*; &
so the *Saints* do aduise. And they say,
that *spirituall Reading*, must be like the
drinking of a Hen, which drinkes by
little, and little, and so lifteth vp the
head agayne.

Heerby a man may see, what a Sister, & Companiō, *Reading* is to *Prayer.*
It is so, in so great degree, that when
we apply any man first to *Mentall Pray-*
er, and that, we will proceed with him
gently (by degrees)to put him into
some disposition that way; we aduise
him *to read some spirituall booke*, & whilst
he is *Reading*, to make some stations &
pawses, in such sort as we haue said;
for by this meanes, our Lord is wont ,
many times, to raise men, to the *Exercise*

Bern. epist.
seu Tract.
ad Fratr.
de monte
Dei. Hau-
riendus
est sæpe
lectionis
seriæ af-
fectus, &
formanda
oratio
quæ le-
ctionem
interrum-
pat, & nō
tam im-
pediat in-
terrum-
pendo.
quâm pu-
riorem
continuo
animum
ad intelli-
gentiam
lectionis
restituat.
Et in spec.
menachor.
Nec sem-
per ad o-

of

ratorium
est eun
dum, sed
in ipsa le-
ctione po-
terit con-
templari
& orare.
*Idem S.
Ephrem.
serm 7.
Chrysost.
ho.10 su-
per Gene-
sim. Aug.
ser. 38. ad
Fra. in e-
remo.*

of Mentall Prayer. And so also, whe men
are not able to enter wel vpon *Prayer,*
and if they thinke they shall not be
able to go through with it, at that
tyme; we vse to counsell them, to take
some good booke in hand, & to ioyne
Prayer, & *Reading* both together. First,
Reading a little, & then *Meditating,* and
Praying vpon it; and then to *Read* another little. For by this meanes, the vnderstanding being tyed vp by the
words, which are read, a man is much
more secured from scattering himselfe
vpon diuers imaginatiõs, & thoughts,
then when he was free, and loose. So
that in *Reading,* we may also very wel,
haue *Prayer.*

Note.

For this it is, that the *Saints* do so
earnestly recommend *spirituall Reading,*
& they deliuer in effect, the same prai-
ses, & profits as belonging to it, which
they ascribe to *Priaer.* For they say, *That
it is the spirituall foode of the soule; That it
makes vs strong & stiffe against temptations;*
*That it breeds in vs, good thoughts, & desires
of heauen. That it giues lighte to our vnderstanding; That it kindles & inflames our wil;
That it driues away the sorrowes of this
world,*

Note.

World, and causeth a ioyfullnes in vs, whichis true and spirituall, & according to God. And such other things as these, they say her-of.

The blessed *S. Bernard* giues vs ano-ther aduertisemét, to make vs profit by *Spiritual Reading.* He saith, *Si ad legendum accedat, non tam quærat scientiã, quàm sapo-rem.* He who comes to Reading, is not so much to seeke knowledge, as a cer-tayne sauour, & gust of the will. For the single knowledge of the *Vnderstan-ding,* is but a dry kinde of thing, if it be not applyed to the *will,* in such sort, as that the affect may, by degrees, be také, and deuotion conserued; for this is that which maketh *Reading* to be full of iuyce, & profit, and it is the *End* therof. This is a very principall aduise. For there is a great deale of difference, be-tween *Reading* to *know;* & *Reading* with a designe to profit, by it; Betwene *Rea-ding* for others, and *Reading* for a mans self. For the former of these two, is *Stu-dy,* & the later is *Spirituall Reading.* And therfore, if whé you dispose your selfe to *Read,* you only direct your mind, to the *Knowing* of things, or to draw out

conceits,

Q 4

Note.

*Bernard.
in speculo
Monacho-
rum.*

côçeits, which you may *preach*, & powre out to others afterward; this should be *studying* for them, and not *Spirituall Reading* for your own profit. For that other, there are other tymes appoynted.

Omnia tempus habent: *Euery thinge hath his tyme*. And the tyme of *spirituall Reading*, is not for *Study*, but for that, which we haue said.

The Saints do also recommēd to vs, for the same reason, That we must not read too much at once, nor passe many howers together therein, least a mans spirit be tired with *long Reading*, insteed of being recreated. Which is another aduise very good, & very necessary, for some, who seeme to place their felicity in *Reading* much, & passing ouer many bookes. But, as much eating is not the thinge which susteynes the body, but good digestion of that which is eaten; so nether is the soule susteined by *Reading* much, but by ruminating, and digesting well, that which is *Read*.

For the same cause, they also say, that *spirituall Reading* must not be, of things very hard; but they must be playne, & rather of deuotion, then difficult. For

things

things of difficulty, are wont to weary the mind, and to dry vp deuotion.
Hugo of *S.Victor,* bringeth an example
of a seruant of God, who was admo-
nished by *Reuelation*, that he should
leaue the *Reading* of such things; and
should resort to the *Liues*, and *Martyr-*
doms of *Saints,* and such other plaine &
deuout writings, wherby he profitted much. S. Bernard sayth further. *Sed*
& de quotidiana lectione, aliquid quotidie in
ventrem memoriæ dimittendum est, quod fi-
delius digeratur;& rursus reuocatum, cre-
brius ruminetur ; quod proposito conueniat,
quod intentioni proficiat, quod detineat ani-
mum,ita vt aliena cogitare non libeat. We
are alwayes to commit somewhat to
our memory of what we *read;* to the
end that we may ruminate, & digeste
it the better afterward; and especially
that, which we see may help vs most,
and wherof we haue most need;to the
end that betweene the howers of the
day, we may go thinking vpon good
and holy things, and not vpon such,
as are impertinent and vayne.

Iust so, as we must not eate, our corporall food, to the end that we may
spend

Hugo de
S. Victore
li.5.erudit.
Didascali-
ca.c. 7.

Bernard.
Epist.seu
tract.ad
fratrem de
monte Dei.

Note.

spend that tyme in eating; but that, in
vertue of the same foode, which then
we take, we may labour all the day.
Now *Reading*, is the *meat*, and spirituall foode of our soule, because they
are the words of God which we *Read*;
and we must not only *Read*, that we
may spend that tyme well in *Reading*,
Note. but to the end that we may profit by
it, all the day after. It will also be very
well done, and it will giue vs great
help towards all goodnes, that we lift
vp our hart, to God, and desire grace
of him; to the end that it may be profitable to vs, and that the things which
we *Reade*, may go imbruing, and ba-
thing the very rootes of our hart: and
that we may remayne more tenderly
affected to vertue, and more *vnbeguiled*
concerning the vanity of the world; &
resolued vpon those things, which import, vs most. And so we read of the
Gregorius. blessed *S. Gregory*, that before he went to
Reade, he euer prepared himselfe by
Psal. 118. 115. *Prayer*; and vsed to say this verse, *Decli-
nate a me maligni, & scrutabor mandata Dei
mei.* Departe from me, you maligne
spirits, for I will consider the law, and
Com-

Commaundements of my God.

To the end, that we may more esteeme of this kind *of Reading*, & animate our selues more therunto, the *Saints* go comparing it, *with hearing the word of God preached.* And they say, that though *Reading* haue not that force, which the *liuing voice* hath, yet doth it enioy other commodityes, which *Sermons* haue not. For first, a man cannot alwayes haue a *Preacher* at hand, as he may haue a *good booke.* Secondly, the good speach of a *Preacher*, passeth through myne ears at once, & workes not therfore, so great effect in me. But that which is well said, in a *good booke*, I may reflect vpon, and reuolue it in my mind by *Reading* it, once, or twice agayne; and by ruminating, and pondering it, and so it will grow to make a great impression in me. Thirdly, by *Reading* in a good booke, I haue a free, and faythfull counsellor. And that other *Philosopher*, said well: *That which, many times, my friend, or my counsellor will not venter to tell me, my booke tells me plainly, without feare, aduertising me of my vices, and defects, and chiding me on the one side, and exhor-*

Note.

Demetrius Phaler.

exhorting me on the other. Fourthly, by this *Reading* I am conuerfing with them, who wrote the booke.

Sometymes you may go, and haue a tyme of conuerfation with *S. Bernard,* another with *S. Gregory* another with *S. Bafill;* and you may ftand hearing, & liftning to them, as truly, as if you had beene their difciple of old tyme. And fo they fay, and with great reafon, *That good bookes, are a kind of publique treafure,* for the great benefits and riches, which we may drawe from thence. To conclude, the profit and aduantage which groweth vpon this *Reading of fpirituall bookes,* is fo very great, that *S. Hierome,* treating of that interior *inflammation* of the foule, doth aske where this *inflamation,* and fire is? And he anfwereth, that there is no doubt to be made, but that it is conteyned in *holy Scriptures, the Reading wherof, inflames the foule, towards God, and fo it remaineth purged from all vice.* And he bringeth, for proofe of this, that which the difciples faid to one another, whé going to the Caftle of *Emans,* Chrift our Lord appeared to them, in forme of a *Pilgrime,* and went

Hieron. epift. ad Damafum Papam.

fpea-

speaking to them of holy Scripture. *Luc.24.*
Nonne cor nostrum ardens erat in nobis, cùm *32.*
loqueretur in via, & aperiret nobis Scriptu-
ras? Was not (say they) our hart all inflamed and in fire, whē he went speaking and declaring the holy Scripture
to vs, vpon the way? And he also
bringeth those words of the Prophet.
Eloquia Domini, eloquia casta, argentum igne *Ps.11.7.*
examinatum; The words of our Lord,
are chast wordes, and pure; they are
as siluer, purifyed by the fire.

And *S. Ambrose* affirmeth, That this
sacred lection, is the life of the soule, *Ambros.*
by the testimony of Christ our Lord *35. ser.*
himselfe. *Quod autem sacrarum litterarū*
lectio vita sit, Dominus testatur dicens, Ioan-
nis sexto, Verba quæ ego locutus sum vobis, *Ioan. 6.*
spiritus & vita sunt. The wordes which *64.*
I haue sayd to you, are spirit & life.
To the end therfore, that we may lead
a *spirituall life*, and that we may walke
euer on, in *true spirit*; & be all kindled,
and inflamed with the Loue of God,
let vs giue our selues much to this
kind of *Sacred Lection*; and let vs vse it
in such sorte, as hath been said.

Now by that, which you haue
seene,

seene, it will follow; That they do very ill, who as soone as they haue *Read* ouer any good booke, do cast it into some corner, and say, *I haue dispatched that booke.* A good booke is not to be read ouer, only once. The second tyme that you read it, will profit you more then the first; and the third, then the second. Yea and it wilbe euer new to you, as they finde by experience, who desire to profit by *Reading.* And it is a good custome which some haue, who when they meete with any thing in any booke which moues them much, and giues them particuler satisfaction, do note it, and set it downe; to the end that they may always haue at hand some of the most substantiall things, and wherein they may finde the iuyce of deuotion, at more ease; & may haue some comfort in store for such occasions, and tymes as may occurre.

Note. We might bring many *Examples,* in confirmation of the great benefit & profit, which groweth from the *Reading of Spirituall bookes*; but I will only bring the Example of *S. Augustine,* which

August. li.8. confess. c. 6.

which conteyneth much doctrine. That *Saynt* recounts, how a certaine *Cauallier*, an *Affrican*, called *Potitianus*, comming one day to visite him, gaue him newes of the wonderfull things, which the world was saying of *S. Anthony*. And he added further, that one euening, while the was at *Treuers*, (imployed, vpon seing certayne publique sports, which were represented there) himselfe with three other *Courtiers*, friends of his, went out to take the aire. And that two, of the sower, did chance vpon the *Cell* of a certaine *Monke*; and finding there a booke, wherein the Life of *S. Anthony* was written, one of them began to read it, and instantly his hart was kindled with a holy kinde of loue. And being all angry with himselfe, he said thus to his friend. *Tell me I beseech thee, what is that which we pretend to obteyne, with all the paines we take? What is that, which we ayme at? In the hope of what, do we thus earnestly imploy our selues? Can we perhaps, haue a higher ambition in the Court, then to be Fauorites of the Emperor? And yet euen in that fortune, what is there, which is not top full of*
                          danger?

danger? And by how many dangers, do we still proceed towards some greater danger? And how long shall we sweat in this pursuite? But to be the friend and fauourite of God himselfe, behold I am made so, if I will, euen at this very instant.

This he said, and being growne bigge, and swolne, with the feruent desire of bringing forth a new life, he restored his eyes to the booke, and read on, and was inwardly changed, and his mind was wholy dispossessed of worldely cares, as immediately afterwards appeared. For whilst he was Reading, and rowling vp and downe, those waues of his vnquiet hart, he would sometymes groane deepely, and then agayne pawse a while. And resoluing at last, vpon a better course, he said with a serene countenance, to his friend: Euen now haue I broken loose, from those hopes wherby hitherto we haue beene seized. I haue firmely resolued, to be the seruant of God, and I will set vpon it, in this place, and at this very instant. As for thee, if thou canst not be content, to imitate me, at least disswade me not. But the other answered, that he would gladly ioyne himselfe to him, as a copanion in the prosecuting of so honorable a war, & the obteyning of so noble a pay. And

both

both of them, did build vp that Spirituall Tower, with the treasure which is only able to do it, of forsaking all things, and following Christ *our Lord.* And that which is as strange, *they both had Spouses, who, as soone as they knew what these men had resolued, did consecrate themselues to God, by a vow of Chastity.*

This doth S. *Augustine* relate ; and this Example was of so great efficacy, with himselfe, that soone after, he thus cryed out, with great exclamation, to another friend of his, *What is this which we indure? What is this? What haue we heard?* Surgunt indocti, & cælum rapiunt, & nos cum doctrinis nostris, sine corde ecce vbi volutamur in carne & sanguine: *The vnlearned men of the world, teare heauen from betweene our hands, and we, with our great knowledge, and learning, behold how without braynes, or courage, we are contented still to wallow, in flesh and blood.*

But with this alteration, and feeling, the Saint relates, *how he entred into a Garden, there adioyning, and did spread himselfe, at the foote of a certaine figtree; and (letting loose the reynes to teares)*

R   *he*

he beganne , with great affliction , and sorrow of hart , to cry out thus to God, and say: And thou , O Lord. how long ? How long, O Lord? Wilt to be angry with vs for euer ? Remember not Lord , our old iniquityes . And still he repeated these words. How long; How long: shall I say, To morrow ? Why not euen now ? Why , euen at this instant , is there not an end of my vncleanenesse ? Whilest he was saying this , in the most bitter feeling of his hart , he heard a voyce which sayd to him. Take vp and read , Take vp and read . He then rose vp (as himselfe relateth) to take vp and read, in that holy booke, which lay before him ; For he had heard it related of the same *S. Anthony* , that by once *Reading* of the *Gospell* , (which he fell vpon) as it were by chance which sayd , *Goe and sell all that thou haste , and giue it to the poore , and follow me , and thou shalt haue treasure in heauen* ; he determined to leaue all things , and to follow *Christ our Lord-*

And so *S. Augustine* , being moued much by this *Example* , & more by the *voyce* , which he had heard, sayth , That he toooke vp the booke , and read in it . And there did God infuse,

Matt. 19, 21,

fo

so great a light into his soule, that leauing all things of this world, he deliuered himselfe wholy vp to the seruice of our Lord.

The end of this Treatise
of Mentall Prayer .

R 2

A TREATISE
Of the presence of God:

Written by the same Authour.

CHAP. I.

Of the excellency of this Exercise: and the great benefits, which are conteyned therein.

QVAERITE Domi-
nam, & confirmami-
ni; quærite faciem
eius semper. Seeke
God (sayth the
Prophet *Dauid*,)
with perseueran-
ce, and strength; be euer seeking his
face: the *face our Lord*, which as *S. Augustine* sayth, is the *Presence of our Lord*;
and

Psa.104.
4.

*August.
super Psal.
104.*

R 3

and so to be euer seeking the *face of our Lord*, *is to be euer going in his* Presence, and conuerting our harts to him, with *desire*, and *loue* .

Isychius.
Bonau. to.
2. opusc. li.
2 de profe-
Ctu Reli-
giosorum.
ca.20.

     Isychius, in his last *Century* sayth, & so doth also *S. Bonauenture* ; *That to be alwayes performing this Exercise of the Presence of God* , *is to begin to be bleßed here on earth, as the glorious spirits are*, *in heauen*. For the felicity of those *Saints* , consisteth in *seeing God* perpetually, without euer once loosing the sight of him. But now, since we cannot *see God* in perfect charity, nor *as he is in himselfe* (for this is only proper to those glorious spirits) yet at least, let vs imitate them , the best we can , according to the vttermost of our frailty; and let vs procure, to be allwayes beholding, respecting, and louing him. So that, as our Lord God created vs , to be eternally in his presence, & to enioy him in heauen; so was it also his pleasure, that, here on earth, we should haue an image, & modell of that blessednesse, by walking euer in his sight, reuearing , and beholding him, though in obscure manner. *Videmus nunc per spe-*
culum

2. Cor. 13.
12.

culum in ænigmate, tunc autem, facie ad faciem. We now behold, and see God, by fayth, as in a glasse; but afterwards, we shall see him cleerely, and face to face. *Ista est meri.um illa præmium.* That cleere vision, (as sayth *Isychius*) is the reward; and the glory and blessednes for which we hope; this other obscure sight, is matter of merit to vs, wherby we must growe to obteyne that other.

But yet still, in fine, we must imitate those blessed spirits, to the best of our power; whilst we procure not to loose the sight of God, in the workes which we are doing. Iust so, as the holy Angells, who are sent downe to our succour, for our defence, and help; are, in such sort imployed vpon those ministeryes, as that yet withall, they neuer loose the sight of God. As the Angell Raphael said to Toby, *Videbar quidem vobiscum manducare, & bibere; sed ego cibo inuisibili, & potu, qui hominibus videri non potest, vtor.* I seemed indeed, to haue beene eating, and drinking with you; but I, the while, did serue my selfe of an inuisible meate, and of a kind of drinke, which cannot be discerned by

Tob.12.13.
Mat.18.
10.

R 4 hu-

humaine eyes. They are euer ſuſtey-
ning themſelues vpon God; *ſemper vi-*
dent faciem patris mei, qui in cælis eſt. And
ſo alſo, although we eate and drinke,
and conuerſe, and negotiate with mē;
and though it ſeeme, that we enter-
teyne, and imploy our ſelues therein,
muſt yet procure, that, that be not our
foode, and entertaynement; but another food and entertaynement, which
is inuiſible, and which men diſcouer
not; and this is, *That we be euer beholding,*
and louing God, and accompliſhing his moſt
boly will.

Great was the accounte, and prae-
ctiſe which the *Saints,* and the ancient
Patriarches made, of going alwayes *in*
Pſa.15. 8. *the Preſence of God Prouidebam Dominum*
in conſpectu meo ſemper; quoniam à dextris
eſt mihi, ne commouear. The *Royall Prophet*
did not content himſelfe, with prai-
ſing God ſeauen tymes in the day; but
withall he procured to haue God alwayes preſent with him. And ſo continuall was this *Exerciſe*, with thoſe
Saynts, that this was alſo their common phraſe of ſpeach, *Viuit Dominus, in*
3. Reg. 17. *conſpectu cuius ſto.* Our Lord liueth, in
whoſe

whose presence I am.

The benefits, and profits are great, which flowe from our going conti-nually *in Gods Presence*, whilst we con-sider that he is euer looking on vs; and therefore did the *Saynts* labour in it so much. This alone, sufficeth to make, that a man be very well ordered, and composed in all his actions. For tell me, what seruant is there, who will not carry himselfe exactly well, vnder the eye of his Lord? Who will not do that which he commaunds? or who will dare to offend him to his teeth? Or what theefe will presume to steale, whilst the Iudge hath an eye vpon his hands?

Now therfore, since God is *so euer looking vpon* vs, and since he is our Iud-ge, and since he is *Omnipotent*, and can commaund that the earth may open and swallowe a man vp into Hell; Yea, and since he hath indeed done so sometymes, to such as durst offend him, what is he, that will dare to offend him any more? And so *S. Augustine* sayth; *O Lord when I consider with atten-tion, that thou art euer looking vpon me, and*
that

4.*Reg*.3. 14.

Note.

Aug.sol. 14.

that thou art watching ouer me, *night and*
day; and that, *with so great care, as if there*
were neither in heauen, nor earth, any other
creature for thee to gouerne, but me alone;
When I consider well, *that all my deeds, de-*
sires, and thoughts, lye open and cletre before
thee, I am all fulfilled with feare, *and ouer-*
whelmed with shame. Without doubt, we
are cast into a very streight obliga-
tion, of liuing with great rectitude, &
iustice, by the consideration of our doing all things, vnder the eye of that
Iudge, who seeth all things, and from
whome, nothing is able to hide it selfe. If in this world, the presence of a
graue, and qualifyed person, will keep
vs in order, what will not the *Presence*
of God be able to do?

S. *Hierome*, vpon that place, where
God said to *Hierusalem*, by the *Prophet*
Ezechiel, *Meiq̃ oblita es*, Thou hast forgotten me, sayth thus; *Memoria enim Dei,*
excludit cuncta flagitia. The memory of
God dismisseth, and dischargeth all
sinne. The same also doth S. *Ambrose*
say. And els where S. *Hierome* sayth a-
gaine. *Certè quando peccamus, si cogitare-*
mus Deum videre, & esse præsentem, num-

quam

Ezech. 22.
28,

quàm quod ei displiceret faceremus. The memory of God and the watching still in
his Presence, is a meanes of so great efficacy, that if we did but consider that
God is present, and doth behold vs,
we would neuer aduenture to do that
thing, which might displease him.
This alone, sufficed to make that sin-
full woman *Thais*, giue ouer her bad
life, and betake herselfe to a course of
pennance, in the wildernes. Holy Iob
said thus: *Nonne ipse considerat vias tuas, &*   Iob. 31. 4.
cunctos greßus meos dinumerat? God stands
beholding me, and as a true ey-witnes
counts the paces which I make; and
who then is that man, who will presume to sinne, or to do any thing
amisse?

On the other side, all the disorder,   Note.
and perdition of the wicked, doth
proceed from their not considering,
that God is *Present*, & beholdeth them;
according to that which the *holy Scri-*
pture doth so often repeate, in the per-   Isa. 47. 10.
son of wicked men: *Et dixisti, non est qui*   Ierem.12.
videat me. Et non videbit nouissima nostra.   4.
And so did S. *Hierome* note it, vpon   Hierome.
the seauenth *Chapter* of *Ezechiel*; where
the

the Prophet, reproouing *Ierusalem* for
the many vices, and sinnes, which it
was subiect to, growes to say, *That the
cause of them all, was for that, that City
had forgotten God.* And he assigneth also the same cause, whe he interpreteth
many other places of *scripture.* For as
a horse without a bridle, and a ship
without a sterne runs vpon precipi-
ces,and rockes ; so if you take this bridle, out of the mouth of man, he runs
headlong after his owne inordinate
appetites, and passions. *Non est Deus in
conspectu eius, inquinatæ sunt viæ illius in
Psa.9.26. omni tempore,*sayth the Prophet,*Dauid.*He
carrieth not God before his eyes, he
considereth him not, as present before
him,and therefore are his ways(which
are his workes) all defiled still, with
sinnes.

The remedy, which the blessed *S.*
Note. *Basil* giues, in many places of his workes, against all temptations, and troubles, and for all the occasions and necessityes, which may present themselues, is the *Presence of God.* And therfore,ifthou desire, a ready, and compendious way,for the obteyning of
perfe-

perfection, and which may conteyne,
and lock vp,in it felfe, the force & efficacy of all other meanes, this is that.
And for fuch, did God giue it thus to *Gen.17.1.*
Abraham; Ambula coram me , & esto perfe-
ctus; Walke before me, & thou fhalt be
perfect. The holy Scripture doth
here, (as in many other places)take the
Imperatiue , for the *Future*, to expreffe
home, the infallibility of the fucceffe.
It is so certaine, that thou shalt be perfect, if
alwayes thou wilt goe beholding of God, and
considering that he is euer beholding thee; that
euen, from this instant, thou maist account,
that thou shalt be perfect. For iuft, as the
Stars do, from the afpect of the *Sunne*
with is prefent to them , draw light ,
wherby they are refplendent, both,
within , and without their owne *bo-*
dyes ; and do alfo get other vertues,
wherby they make influence vpō the
earth ; fo do iuft, and vertuous men
(who are as fo many *stars* in the *Church*
of God)from the fight of God, and by
confidering him *euer prefent* , and by
conuerting their thoughts and defires
to him , draw light , wherby in their
interior, (which God fees) they fhine
with

with reall, & folide vertues; & in their exteriour, (which men fee) they fhine with all innocency, and decency; and they draw ftrength , and force from thence, for the edification, and profit of others.

There is nothing in the whole world , which doth fo properly declare the neceffity that we haue , of continuing euer in the *Prefence* of God, as this which followes. Behould the dependance, which the *Moone* hath vpon the *Sun*; & the neceffity, to which it is fubiect , of being euer in prefence of it. The *Moone*, of it felfe, hath no clarity, but receiues it all from the *Sunne*, according to the proportion of the afpect , which it hath from thence. And it worketh vpon inferiour bodyes, according to the rate of clarity, which it receaues from the *Sunne* ; and fo do the effects therof, increafe or faile, according to the *full*, or *wayning* of the fame light. And when any thing doth place it felfe aboue the *Moone* , which may depriue it of the fight, & view of the *Sunne*, at that inftant , is the luftre and clarity therof *ecclipfed* ; & therewith

Note.

withall, a great part also failes, of the
efficacy, which it had to worke, by
meanes of the *Sunne*. Now in the selfe
same manner, doth it passe betweene
the *soule*, and *God*, who is the true *Sunne*
of the *soule*.

For this cause it is, that the *Saynts*,
do so earnestly recommend this *Exercise* to vs. *S. Ambrose*, and *S. Bernard* dis-
courling of the continuance, & perse-
uerance which we are to vse herein,
say thus; *Sicut nullum est momentum, quo* *Amb.lib.*
homo non vtatur, vel fruatur Dei bonitate & *de dignita-*
misericordia; sic nullum debet esse momentum, *te con.*
quo eam prasentem non habeat in memoria.
As there is no pointe, or moment of
tyme, wherein man enioyeth not the
goodnesse and mercy of God; so ought
there not to be any pointe, or moment of tyme, wherein he ought not
to haue God present to him, in his memory. And *S. Bernard* sayth els where.
In omni actu, vel cogitatu suo, sibi Deum
adesse memoretur ; & omne tempus , quo de
ipso non cogitat , perdidisse se computet. A
Religious man, must procure , in all
his thoughts, and in all his deeds , to
remember that he hath God present
with

with him; and all that tyme, wherein he thinketh not of God, he is to hold for loſt. God doth neuer forget vs, & it is but reaſon, that we procure to be neuer vnmindfull of him.

S. *Auguſtine*, vpon the 31. *Pſalme*, *Firmabo ſuper te oculos meos*, ſayth: *Non à te auferam oculos meos, quia & tu non aufers à me oculos tuos.* I will not, O Lord, withdraw myne eyes from thee, becauſe thou doſt not withdraw thine eyes from me. Continually, will I lodge them fixed, & firme vpon thee, as thy Prophet did, who ſaid: *Oculi mei ſemper ad Dominum* ; Mine eyes are euer vpon our Lord. S. *Gregory Nazianzen* ſayth : *Non tam ſæpe reſpirare, quàm Dei meminiſſe debemus* ; As often ought we to remember God, yea and more often, then we fetch our breath. For as we haue need of reſpiration, for the refreſhing of our harts, and for the tempering of our naturall heat; ſo are we in continuall neceſſity, of reſorting to God, by *Prayer*, for the reſtraint of that inordinate heate of concupiſcence, which is mouing and intiſing vs to ſinne.

Aug. Pſa. 31. 8.

Pſ. 24. 15.

Gregor. Naz. in ora. Theologica.

CHAP.

CHAP. II.

Wherein consisteth the Exercise , or Practise of going alwayes , in the Presence of God.

TO the end that we may serue our selues the better, of this exercise, or practise, it wilbe necessary to declare wherin it consists . It consisteth in two *Acts* ; the one is, of the *Vnderstanding,* the other is of the *Will.* The first *Act,* is of the *Vnderstanding.* For this is euer requisite and presupposed , for the performing , of any act of the *Will,* as we are taught by *Philosophy.* The first thing therfore, is to be, to consider with the *Vnderstanding ,* *That God is both heere, & euery where els. That he filleth the whole world, and that he is all, in all in euery parte , and in euery creature , how small soeuer it may be .*

Of this , an *Act* is to be made, because this is a certayne *Truth,* which *Fayth* propoundeth to be belieued by *Vs. Non enim longe est ab vnoquoq, nostrum; in ipso enim viuimus , mouemur, & sumus ;* sayth

Noted

Tract. 5. *cap.* 7.

Act. 17. 17.

S

sayth the Apostle *S. Paul.* You are
not to imagine, or fansy God, as one
who were farre from you; or as if he
were *without* you; for he is *within* you.

Confeʃʃ. l.
10. c. 27. *S. Augustine* confesseth thus, *I ʃough that*
without me, O Lord, which yet was within
me. Within you is God; and more *pre-*
ʃent, and more intrinsecally, & more
intimately is God in me, then my selfe.
In him we liue, and moue, and haue our being.
He it is, who giueth *Life*, to all that
which *liues*; and he, who giueth *ʃtrēgth*
to all which hath any *ʃtrength*; and he
who giues *being*, to all that which *is.*
And if he were not *preʃent*, suʃteyning
all things, they all would leaue to be,
and returne to their *nothing.* Conʃidet
therfore, that thou art all, full of God;
inuironed & compaʃʃed in with God,
and as it were ʃwimming in God. *Ple-*
ni ʃuunt cæli & terra gloria tua, are very
good wordes to this purpoʃe: *The hea-*
uens, and the earth, are full of thy glory.

Note.   Some, to help themʃelues, more in
this, do conʃider all the world to be
full of God, as indeed it is; and they
imagine themʃelues, to be in the mid-
deʃt of this infinite *ʃea of God*; circled, &
hemmed

hemmed in by him, in such sort, as a
sponge, in the middest of the *sea* might
be, all bathed, and full of water, and
besides compassed in, and enclosed by
water, on all sides. This comparison is
not ill, for the rate of our weake vnderstanding. But yet it falleth short, &
reacheth not, by a great deale, to declare that, wherof we are speaking. For
that *Sponge,* in the middest of the *Sea,* if
it mount vpwards, it is at an end, a-
boue; if it descend downeward, it findes an end, below; and it meets with a
stay, if it go eyther on the one side, or
the other; but in God, thou shalt find
nothing, of all this. *Si ascendero in cæ-*
lum, tu illic es; si descendero in infernum ades,
si sumpsero pennas meas diliculo, & habitaua-
ro in extremis maris, etenim manus tua de-
ducet me, & tenebit me dextera tua. If I
mount vp to heauen, thou art there O
Lord; if I descend downe to hell, thou
art also there; if I take wings, and passe
to the extreme sides of the sea, thither
will thy hand carry me, and there thy
right hand will hold me. There is no
end, or terme in God, because he is infinite and immense. Besides, in fine,

since

since the *Sponge* we spake of , is *a body*, it cannot be wholly penetrated, by the *water* ; which is another *Body*; whereas we, are in all , and through all, penetrated by Almighty God, who is *pure spirit*. But yet neuertheles , these comparisons, and the like (how short soeuer they fall , of expressing the thing,) are good , and do giue greate helpe, for the vnderstanding in some sort , of the infinite immensenesse of God, and how he is *present*, & most intimately in vs, and in all things. And therfore , S. *Augustine* bringeth these comparisons.

Epist . 57. ad Darda-num. & l. 7 . Confess. cap, 5.

But yet, we are to obserue in the performance of this *Exercise* of *the Presence of God*, that there is no necessity, to forme any *conceit*, with the *imagination*, or any *representation* at all, of God; feigning that he is here, at our side, or in any other determinate place; or that he is in this, or the other *forme* . There are some, who imagine eyther before themselues , or on the one side that Christ *Iesus* our redeemer, is with the, and that he goes with them , and is euer looking vpon what they do, and is in this manner, they euer go in the *Presence of God.* Of these, some *imagine,* that they haue *Chrift crucifyed* before them; others, that he is tyed to the *Pillar*; others, that he is *sweating* drops of bloud in his *Prayer* of the *Garden* ; others, in some other part of his *Passion*; or els in some cheerefull *myftery* of his moft holy life; euery one, according to his inclination, and deuotion. Or els, some one tyme they imagine him in some one fashion, & at another tyme, in some other.

And although this be very profitable, for such as know how to do it wel; yet (ordinarily speaking) it is not that, which is beft for vs. For all these **Note.** *formes* , and *imaginations* of *corporall things,* do toyle and weary men; and many tymes , do much trouble their heads. A *Saint Bernard,* or *a Saint Bonauenture,* without doubt, knew better how to do this, then we; and they found much facility, and eafe in it; and fo they would be able to go into those holes, of the *wounds* of Chrift our Lord, and into his *holy fide*; and there, would they find their reft, their refuge,

and

and their safe retrayt; esteeming themselues to heare those words of the *spouse*
in the *Canticles*, spoken to themselues:
*Surge amica mea, speciosa mea, & veni; co-
lumba mea in foraminibus petra, in cauerna
maceria.* At other tymes, they would
imagine the foote of the *Crosse*, to be
fastned and rooted in their *harts* , and
that they, the while, were receiuing by
their mouth, with extreme sweetnes,
those drops of *bloud*, which ran , and
streamed from those fountaines, of the
Sauiour of the world. *Haurietis aquas in
gaudio, de fontibus Saluatoris.* Those *Saints*
I say, did very well, in doing thus, and
they were happy in it; but if you will
be going on, all day, in these considerations, and with this kind of *Presence
of God*; perhaps, that for one day, or moneth, which you may passe after this
fashion, you will loose your *Prayer* for
a whole yeare. For it may cost you ,
the breaking of your braynes.

    We may see how great reason there
is, why we should be carefull, in giuing this lesson of caution , since euen
for making a kind of *structure* or *compo-
sition of place*, (which is one of the *Preambles*

Isa. 12. 3.

Note.

bles , or *Preludes* of *Prayer*, wherby we
are wont to make that matter prefent to vs, wherof we are to meditate,
imagyning that the matter doth really
paffe before vs there) they who treat of
Prayer, are carefull to aduertife vs, that
we do not, with an attention too
much bent, fix our imagination vpon
the *figure*, or *reprefentation* of thofe *corporall things*, wherof we meane to
thinke, for the danger, which there is
to breake our braynes ; and for other
inconueniéces, of *illufions*, which grow
fometymes out of this roote. If therfore, for the making of a *Preamble*, or
Prelude of *Prayer*, (which vfeth to be
paffed ouer, fo very foone, and the
man, being at that tyme, in quietnes,
and at good leafure, without hauing
any other thing to poffeffe his mind,)
there be need of fo much circumfpe-
ction, and caution; what will there be,
for one who hath a mind to conferue
this kind of *compofition*, for the whole
day, and in the middeft of all his other
bufineffe ?

But now, this other *Prefence of God*,
wherof we treate, excludes all thefe

S 4 *imagi-*

imaginations, & indeed is very far from them all. For now we treate, of a *Presence of God, as God* And firſt, we need not feigne to our ſelues, that he is here; but we muſt beleeue it, for ſo he is indeed. *Chriſt our Lord, as man*, is in *heauen*, and in the *B. Sacrament* of the *Altar*; but he is not euery where. And therfore, when we imagine, Chriſt our Lord, as man, to be preſent with vs, it is an *imagination*, and a thing which we faigne to our ſelues. But now, as God, he is *preſent* heer; and he is within me, and he is in all places, & he fills them all. *Spiritus Domini replauit orbem terra-*

Sap. 1. 7.

rum. We haue no cauſe, in this caſe, to feigne, that which is not; but to actuate our minds in the firme, & frequent belieſe, of that which is.

Secondly, the humanity of Chriſt our Lord, may be fancied, and figured by the *imagination*, becauſe he hath a body, and a figure; but God, as God, cannot be *imagined*, or figured, as he is, becauſe he hath no *body*, nor *figure*, but is *a pure ſpirit*. Nay we cannot ſo much as imagine an *Angell*, no nor *our owne ſoule*, as indeed it is, becauſe it is a *ſpirit*;

and

and how much lesse then, shall we be
able to imagine, or frame a conceit
of, how God is.

But how then, are we to confider,
that God as God, is still *prefent* with
vs? I fay there is no more to be done,
but only to produce an act of *Fayth*,
fuppofing already, that God is *prefent*
there; fince our *Fayth* tells vs fo, without labouring to know how, or in
what fafhion that is; as *S. Paul* affir-
mes, that *Moyfes* did. *Qui inuifibilem, tan-*
quam videns, fuftinuit. He confidered *God,*
who is inuifible, and had him prefent ftill, as
if he had feene him. But yet fo, as that he
would not ftriue to know, or *ima-*
gine, how that was; but, as when a mã
is fpeaking with fome friend of his, by
night, without reflecting how that is,
and not confidering it; but only re-
ioycing, and delighting in the conuerfation and prefence of his friend,
who he knowes is prefent, with him
there. In this fort, are we to confider
God *prefent* with vs. It is inough that
we know, our frend is there, that we
may enioy him. Do not dwell vpon
thinking, how that is. You will not
light

Note!

light vpon it; for it is yet, by night, for
vs. Do but ſtay till it be light , and
when the morning of the other life
appeares; he will then be diſcouered,
and we ſhalbe able *to ſee him cleerely,
as he is. Cùm apparauerit, ſimiles ei erimus,
quoniam videbimus eum ſicuti eſt.* For this,
did God appeare to *Moyſes,* in obſcuri-
ty, and in a cloud ; that you may not
looke to *ſee* him, but only *belieue* him
to be preſent.

All this which we haue ſaide, belongs to the firſt act of *Vnderſtanding,*
which muſt be preſuppoſed. But it
muſt be conſidered alſo heere, that the
chiefe part of this *Exerciſe* , doth not
conſiſt in this . For not only is the
Vnderſtanding to imploy it ſelfe , in
behoulding God *preſent* ; but a man
muſt alſo imploy the *Will;* by aſpiring
to God, and by louing him, and by
vniting himſelfe to him. And in theſe
acts of the *Will,* this *Exerciſe* doth principally conſiſt , whereof we ſhall
treate, in the next Chapter.

CHAP.

CHAP. III.

Of the acts of the Will, wherein this Exercise
doth principally consist; and how we are
to imploy our selues therein.

SAINT *Bonauenture*, in his *Mysticall*
Theology sayth, that the *Acts* of the
Will, wherewith we must lift vp our
selues to God, in this holy *Exercise*, are
certayne ardent desires of the hart,
wherby the soule doth thirst, to be v-
nited with God, in *perfect loue*. Certayne *inflamed affections*, they are ; certayne
sighes, which breake out of the very
bowells of the soule, wherewith it cals
vpon God. Certayne *pious, and amorous*   Note.
springings of the will, wherewith, as with
certayne *spirituall wings*, she reacheth, &
stretcheth her selfe vpward; and goes
approaching , and vniting herselfe ,
more and more, with God. These desires, these vehement, and enflamed affections of the hart, the Saints do call
Aspirations. Because by them, the soule
raiseth herselfe vp to God, which sig-
nifyeth the same, with *aspiring* towards

wards him. *S. Bonauenture* alſo ſayth, they are therfore called *Aſpirations*, be-cauſe, as by reſpiring we do, without deliberation, draw our breath, & that interior aire of our body; ſo do we alſo with great agility , and ſometymes without any deliberation at all, (or in effect without any) drawe out theſe inflamed deſires, from the moſt inter-nall part of our ſoule.

Theſe *Aſpirations*, and deſires, a man declares by certayne *Prayers*, which are ſhort, and frequent , and they are cal-led *iaculatory* , *Raptim iaculatas*, ſayth *S. Auguſtine*. Becauſe they are as arrowes, or fiery darts , which ſpring from the hart, and at an inſtant they are ſhot of, and ſent vp to God. Thoſe old *Monkes*, according to the relation of *Caſsian*, did much vſe theſe *Prayers. Breues quidem, ſed creberrimæ*. And they eſteemed , and made great account therof : Partely, becauſe they were ſhort, and did not weary the brayne ; and partly, becauſe they were made with feruour, and with an erected ſpirit; and at an inſtant they are ſent into the *high Preſence of Almighty God*, in ſuch ſort, as that the di-

uell hath no tyme to trouble him, that
makes them; nor to cast any impediment into his hart. *S. Augustine* deliuereth certaine words which are worthy
of Consideration, with such, as are in
Exercise of Prayer. *Ne illa vigilans, &
erecta intentio, quæ tamen necessaria est oran-
ti, per productiores moras hebetetur.* Least
that vigilant, and sharpe attention,
(which yet is needfull for him that
meanes to pray, with dew respect, and
reuerence) go not lessing, or loosing it
selfe, as it hapneth sometymes, in long
prayer. With these *iaculatory Prayers*
therfore, did those holy *Monkes*, go euer
on in this *exercise*; lifting vp their harts,
very frequently to God, and treating,
and conuersing with him.

This way, of going in the *Presence of
God*, is (generally speaking) more fit
for vs, more easy, and more profitable.
It will therfore be necessary, to proceed in declaring the vse, and practise
of this *Exercise*. *Cassian* placeth it, in this
verse, which the *Church* repeateth at
euery hower, of her *Diuine Office. Deus
in adiutorium meum intende; Domine ad adiuuandum me festina.* Art thou entring
into

*Aug. ep.
ad Proba.
Chrif.hom.
79.
Abbas I-
faac.collas.
10. cvp.108*

*Cass.collat.
10. cap.10.*

in to any busines, wherein there may
be difficulty, or danger? Desire thus
of God, that he will helpe thee well
out of it, *O Lord be carefull to succour me :*
O Lord be not slacke to giue me help. We are
in need of the fauour of God, for all
things; and so are we, euer to be desiring his assistance. And *Cassian* sayth,
that this verse, is excellent, and highly
to the purpose; for declaring all the affects of our mind, in whatsoeuer state,
and in whatsoeuer occasion, or acci-
dent, we may find our selues. Because
hereby we inuoke the aide of God;
Heerby we humble our selues, and we
acknowledge our necessity and misery; Heerby we raise our selues, and we
confide to be heard, and fauoured by
Almighty God. Hereby we kindle
our selues, in the loue of our Lord,
who is our protection and refuge. A-
gainst all the combats, and temptations, which may present themselues,
you haue heere, a most strong buckler,
an impenetrable coate-armour, and an
inexpugnable wall. And therfore you
are still to be carrying it, both in your
mouth, and in your hart; and this is to
be

Note.

be your conſtant, & continuall *Prayer*; and your way of going ſtill, *in the Preſence of God*.

S. Baſil, placeth the practiſe of this *Exerciſe*, in that, at all tymes, we take occaſion to remember God. Art thou eating? giue thankes to God. Doſt thou cloth thy ſelfe? giue thanks to God. Art thou going to take the aire, or into thy Garden? bleſſe thou God, who made it. Doeſt thou looke vp to heauen? doeſt thou looke towards the *Sunne*? then do thou praiſe the Creatour of all things. When thou goeſt to ſleepe, and whenſoeuer thou doſt wake, lifte vp thy hart to God.

Note

Now foraſmuch, as in ſpirituall lif, there are three wayes, *The Purgatiue way*, which belongeth to *beginners*; the *Illuminatiue way*, which belongeth to ſuch as are *Proficient*; & the *Vnitiue way*, which belongeth to ſuch as are in ſome degree of *perfection*; there are ſpirituall directours, who aſſigne three kinds of *Aſpirations*, or *Iaculatory Prayers*. Some, which are addreſſed towards the obteyning of pardon for ſinne, and towards the purging of the ſoule from

vice,

vice, and terrene affections, which belong to the *Purgatiue way*. Others, which are addreſſed towards the obteyning of *vertues*, and ouercomming temptations, and vndertaking of difficultyes, and troubles, for the exerciſe of piety; which belong to the *Illuminatiue way*. And others, which addreſſe vs, towards the obteyning of an *Vnion* of the ſoule with God, by the bond of perfect loue; and theſe, belong to the *Vnitiue way*. And this they ordayne, to the end that euery one, may imploy himſelfe in that *exerciſe*, which is moſt agreable, and fit for his owne diſpoſition, and ſtate.

Note,

But yet know this the while; that how perfect ſoeuer a man be, he may ſafely exerciſe himſelfe in ſorrow for his ſinnes, and in deſiring pardon of God for them, and begging grace that he may neuer offend him, and this wilbe a very good Exerciſe of his mind, and very acceptable to God. And both he, and that other man, who is ſtill procuring but to *purge* his ſoule from vice, and inordinate affections; & he alſo, who laboureth to obteyne *Vertue,*

tue, may also exeicise himselfe in acts of the *Loue of God,* to make that other *exercise,* which he is chiefly about, more easy and sweete. Therfore all men may imploye themselues, sometymes, in this *purgatiue exercise,* by making such *Acts* as these: *O Lord, that I had neuer offended thee. Do not permit, O my Lord, that euer I may offed thee any more. Let me dye as much as thou wilt, but neuer let me sinne against thee. Let it please thy diuine maiesty, that I may rather die a thousand deaths, then euer commit one mortall sinne.*

At other tymes, one may raise his hart to God, by giuing him thankes for all his benefits, both generall and particuler, which he hath receiued ; or els by begging the gifte of some *vertue*; sometymes profound *humility*; at other tymes *perfect Obedience*; at other tymes, *Patience*; at others, *Charity.*

Agayne, at other tymes, a man may raise his mind to God, by acts of *loue,* and *conformity* to his most holy will, saying this, or the like. *Dilectus meus mihi, & ego illi. Non mea voluntas, sed tua fiat. Quid enim mihi est in calo, & à te quid volui super terram?* These, and such others,

Cant.2.18
Luc.22.
42.
Psa.72.23,

T

thers, are very good *aspirations*, and *iaculatory Prayers*; wherby a man may go
alwayes, in this *exercise* of the *Presence of
God*. And they vse to be the best, and
most efficacious, which the hart, being
moued by Almighty God, doth con-
ceaue within it selfe; although it be not
done, in words, so well composed and
ordered, as those which we haue heere
set downe.

Note.

And there is also, no necessity at all,
that these *iaculatoryes*, should be many,
in number. For one alone, being very
often repeated, and with great ardour
of mind, may suffice a man for the going in this *exercise* may dayes, yea and
euen all his life. If you finde your selfe
well, with alwayes saying those
words of the Apostle, *O Lord what wilt
thou haue me do?* Or those other of the
Spouse, My beloued to me, and I to him: Or
els those words of the *Prophet*, *What
haue I to desire O Lord, in heauen, or in earth,
but only thee?* you haue need of no
more; deteyne your selfe here, and en-
tertayne your seife herein; and let this
be your continuall *Exercise*, and your
going in *the Presence of God*.

Note.

CHAP.

Chap. IV.

The practise of this Exercise *is further de-clared, and heere a way is laid downe, of going in the* Presence *of God, very easy, very profitable, and of much* Perfection.

AMONGST other *Aspirations,* and *Iaculatory Prayers,* which we may vse; that one, is a very principall one, and very much to purpose, for the pra-ctise of this Exercise, which is taught vs, by the *Apostle Saint* Paul, in his first Epistle to the *Corinthians. Siue manduca-tis, siue bibitis, siue aliud quid facitis, omnia ad gloriam Dei facite.* Whether you eate or drinke, or whatsoeuer els you do, let all be done to Gods glory. Procure, in all things that you do, or at least the most frequently that you can, to lift vp your hart to God, saying; *For thee O Lord, do I this. To content thee, and to please thee. Because thou wilt haue it so; Thy will, O my Lord, is mine; Thy contentment is mine; I haue no other will: nor no other not-will, but that only, which thou wilt, and that which thou wilt not. This is all my delight, all my*

1. Cor. 10. 31.

Note.

T 2   *con-*

contentment, all my ioy, the accomplishment of thy will, to please thee; and there is no other thing but this, for which I care; nor which I can desire; nor which is worth, so much, as the looking on, eyther in heauen, or in earth .

This is a good way, of going allwayes in *the Presence of God*, and very easy, and very profitable, and of much perfection. For it is to go, in a continuall exercise of the loue of God. And *Tract. 3. cap. 8. & Tract. 8. cap. 4.* because I haue treated hereof elsewhere, I will only add in this place, that this is one of the best, and most profitable wayes of going euer in *Prayer*, of all the wayes that can be thought. For it seemes, that there wanted no other thing, to extoll and canonize this *Exercise*, but only to say, that by it, we shalbe in that continuall *prayer*, which Christ our Lord demaunds of vs, in the holy *Gospell*. *Oportet semper orare, & non deficere.* *Luc. 18. 1.* For what better Prayer, can there be, then that one should be euer desiring, the greatest honor, and *glory* of God, and to be euer conforming himselfe, to Gods will. Not hauing any other, eyther will, or not-will, but that which God will,

Will, and willeth not; and that all his
contentment, and ioy, is the contentment, and good pleasure, of our Lord
God.

Therfore sayth a learned Doctour,
and with great reason, that he who
shall perseuere with care, in those affects, and interiour desires, shall reape
so abundant fruite therby, that in short
tyme, he will feele his hart, all conuerted, and changed; and will find therein, a particuler auersion frō the world,
and a singuler affection to Almighty
God. This is to begin already, to be a
kind of Cittizen of heauen, and a standing seruant, in the house of God. *Iam
non estis hospites, & aduenæ, sed estis ciues
Sanctorum, & domestici Dei.* These are
those *Courtiers*, whome *S. Iohn* saw in
the *Apocalyps*, who *carried the name of
God, written in their forheads*, which is the
continuall memory, and Presence of
God. *Et videbunt faciem eius, & nomen
eius in frontibus eorum.* For their conuersation, and discourse, is not now, on
earth, but in heauen. *Nostra autem con-
uersatio in cælis est. Non contemplantibus nobis, ea quæ videntur, sed ea quæ non videntur:*

quæ

T 3

*Dionis. Ri-
chel. l. 1. de
contempla.
cap. 25.*

Eph. 2. 9.

*Apoc. 12.
4.
Philip. 3.
2. Cor. 4.
18.*

*quæ enim videntur temporalia funt, quæ au-
tem non videntur, æterna.*

Note.

It is further to be confidered in this
Exercife, that when we produce thefe
Acts faying: *For thee O Lord, do I this ; For
thy loue; Becaufe thou wilt haue it fo,* &: the
like; we are to do them, and fay them,
as one who fpeakes to God, already
prefent; and not as one, who raifeth his
hart, or his thought, to fend it far off, or
without himfelfe. This aduife is of
great importance in this *Exercife.* For
this is properly, to go in the *Prefence of
God,* and this is that, which makes this
Exercife, eafy, and fweete, and which
makes it moue, and profit more. Yea,
euen in our other Prayers, when we
meditate of Chrift vpon the *Croffe,* or
at the *Pillar;* they who treate of *Prayer,*
giue counfaile, that we fhould not *imagine,* that to be at *Ierufalem,* and that it
paffed, a thoufand, and fo many hun-
dred yeares agoe ; for this wearyes
more, and moues leffe: But we are to
imagine it, as prefent, where we are; &
that it paffeth there before vs; and that
we heare the ftrokes of the fcourges, &
the knocks of the hammers. And if we
medi-

meditate the *Exercise* of *death*; they say
that we are to imagine, that we are
already vpon the point to dye, and
giuen ouer by the *Physitians*; and with
the *holy candle* in our hand. How much
more reason then, shall it be, that in
this *Exercise* of the *Presence of God*, we
performe those *acts*, which we haue
named, not as men, who speake with
an absent person, and that far off from
vs; but as men who speake with God
present; since the very *Exercise* it selfe,
requires it, and in reality of *Truth*, he is
Present.

Chap. V.

*Of some differences. and aduantages, which
there are, in this Exercise, of going in the
Presence of God.*

TO the end that we may the better
see the perfection, and profit of
this *Exercise*, and way of going in the
Presence of God which we haue shewed;
and to the end that it may be the more   Note!
declared, we will touch some differences, and aduantages, which there
T 4   are

are therein. The firſt is this . In the other *Exerciſes* of the *Preſence of God,* which ſome vſe to propound ; all ſeemes to be but an *act* of the *Vnderſtanding*, and all ſeemes to end in this, that they *imagine the Preſence of God.*

But this *Exerciſe*, preſuppoſeth, this *Act* of the *vnderſtanding* . & of *fayth, That God is preſent* and then it goes further on, and maketh *Acts* of the *Loue of God;* and in theſe, it doth principally conſiſt. And this doth euidently appeare, to be better, and more profitable then the former. Iuſt ſo , as we ſaid in the

Tract 5. c. 14.

Treatiſe of Prayer , that we are not to dwell in the *acts* of the *Vnderſtanding*, which is the *Meditation*, and *Conſideration* of things; but in the *acts* of the *Will,* that is, in the *affects* and *deſires* of *vertue*, and the *imitation of Chriſt our Lord* ; and this is to be of the *fruite* of *Prayer*. And ſo heere, the chiefe and beſt, and moſt profitable part of this *Exerciſe* , conſiſts in the *acts* of the *will* ; and this is that, wherupon we muſt inſiſt moſt.

Note.

The ſecond benefit which followes vpon this *Exerciſe* , is that it is more ſweet, and facill, then the reſt. For to

thoſe

those others, is necessary discourse, and
labour of the *vnderstanding*, and *imagination*, to represent *formes* betore it ; which
is the thing, that vseth to weary , and
to breake the braynes , and therfore it
cannot last so longe. Whereas towards
this *Exercise*, there is no neede of *discourse*, but of *affects*, and *acts* of the *will*,
which are produced without difficul-
ty. For although it be true, that there
is some *act* of the *Vnderstanding*, euen
there; yet that, is presupposed by *Fayth*,
without wearying vs therby. And as
when we adore the *B. Sacrament*, we
presuppose by *Fayth*, that Christ our
Lord is *present* there; and all our attention, and imployment is , in adoring ,
reuering, louing, and begging fauours
of that Lord, whome we know to be
present; so it is in this *Exercise*. And from
hence also it is, that the same, being
more facill, one may continue, and
perseuere in it, longer tyme. For euen
to sick persons , who are not capable
of any other *Prayer* , we are wont to
aduise , that they are often to lift vp
their harts to God, with some *affects &
acts* of the *Will*, because they may be
produ-

produced with facility. And therfore,
although there were no other aduantage belonging to this *Exercife*, but only, that one may continue, and perfeuere in it, longer tyme, then in the reſt;
we ſhould haue reaſon, to eſteeme it
much, and therfore how much more,
are we to do it, hauing ſo many aduantages beſides.

The third, and principall thinge, &
that which we are to obſerue very
well, is : That *the Prefence of God* is not
only conſidered, to the end, that we
may dwell in that;but to the end, that
it may ſerue vs, for a meanes to do
thoſe other things well, which we are
to performe. For if we ſhould content
our ſelues, with hauing an attention
to *the prefence of God*, and therby did ne-
glect our workes themſelues, and did
performe them with faults;this would
be no good *deuotion*, but an *illuſion* We
are alwayes to make account, that although we carry one of our eyes towards his diuine Maieſty , we muſt
place the other, vpon the worke it
felfe;that we may performe it well, for
the loue of him. And our ſeeing , that
                                        we

we stand in the *Presence of God*, must be
the meanes , to make vs do all that,
which we are to do , the better, and
with the more perfection. And this, is
much better done by this *Exercise*, then
by others. For in the performing of o-
thers , the *Vnderstanding* is much imployed, about those *corporall figures*,
which a man hath a mynde to set before himselfe , or about those *conceytes*
which he will drawe out of that,
which he hath present to him ; and
whilst he will needs drawe this , or
that good consideration from thence,
many tymes he markes not well, what
he is doing, and so he fails out to do
it ill.

But this *Exercise*, since it busieth not
the *Vnderstanding*, doth not hinder, any
way, the good performance of the
workes; but rather it doth greatly helpe, that they may be exactly done. For
he is doing them, for the loue of God;
and in the *Presence of God*, who lookes
vpon him. And so he procures to do
them, in such sort, and so well, as that
they may be fit to appeare before the
eyes of that diuine Maiesty ; and that
there

there may be nothing therein, which
is vnworthy of his *Presence.* Concerning which, we spake else where, of
another point, which sheweth another way of going in the *Presence of
God,* which is very good and profitable, and recommended by the Saynts
and therfore we will forbeare to repeate it heere.

Chap. VI.

*Certayne pious Considerations, of Gods Im-
mensity, and of his Presence in all places,
and in all things.*

1. **T**O consider that God is so immense and great, as he filleth all
his creatures with his infinite Greatnes, and is more inwardly present in
all things, then they be in their owne
Essence. And notwithstanding all
this, he is not imprisoned heere in the
world: and though there were many
millions of worlds more, yet should
he be still infinitly greater then they,
in so much as it is impossible to fly frō
him, sith he is by his Essence, Presēce,

and

and power in all places; and all creatures be filled with his greatnes. This
confideration fhould make vs more
prefent to our felues in all our actions,
both priuate, and publike, by reprefenting to our felues, that Gods eyes be
vpon vs; and making vnto our felues
an Oratory in all places, fith he is euery where. We muft excite in our felues
affections of ioy, and of admiration, at
fo wonderfull a greatnes.

2.   We muft confider our felues,
as liuing, and doing our actions in
God, who enuironeth vs round, as
doth the water of the Ocean compaffe
in the fifh that fwym, and liue therin.
And this confideration, fhould keep
vs from going and wandring out of
our felues; feeing we haue God prefent within vs, as though we were his
houfe; or by confidering our felues en-
uironed without, & penetrated within by God, as though he were our
owne, and belonging vnto vs.

3.   To confider, how God fhe-
weth himfelfe in heauen to his Elect
with vnuealed, and open face, working in them moft glorious things;
and

and he giueth in some places on earth particuler signes of his presence, as *Iacob* saw him on that mysticall ladder, whereof the Scriptures make mention. God also hath his aboad particulerly in the Churches, and Oratories; and in a more excellent manner in the iust, with whome he abideth by his grace, and worketh strange and wonderfull thinges in them. But aboue all, he is with some great friends of his in this life, producing spiritually within them miraculous effects, as illustrations, discourses of the soule, reuelations of diuine mysteries, which be all signes, and testimonyes of his particular presence. All this ought to make vs the more attentiue, and present to God, and our selues; and more composed both within, and without.

THE COLLOQVY.

O my soule, thou hast within thee all good things, how doest thou not enioy them? Within thee is thy soueraigne freind, and Father; reioyce to haue him with thee: ioyne thee ioyntly with him, and giue vnto him thy whole hart.

hart. If thou art poore, thou hast God with thee, who is rich in mercy, runne vnto him, that he may impart vnto thee of his riches. If thou art weake, and pusillanimous, thou hast God with thee, who is fortitude it selfe; and vnited with him, thou maist doe all things in vertue of him: wherfore then doest thou seeke without thee, with anxietie, helpe of the creatures, hauing within thee, the omnipotency of the Creator? O my Creator, my God, and my all things, perfect in me this strayte coniunction which thou hast with me, vniting thy selfe also with me, by the perfect vnion of grace, that I also may conioyne my selfe with thee, by the perfect vnion of charity. Amen.

FINIS.